Unapologetic Christianity

Bold Living
iN a
CHaotic WorLd

Jamaal Bernard Sr.

Unapologetic Christianity: Bold Living in a Chaotic World

Author: Jamaal Bernard Sr.

Published by Austin Brothers Publishing
Fort Worth, Texas

www.abpbooks.com
ISBN 978-0-9983071-0-7
Copyright © 2016 by Jamaal Bernard Sr.

All biblical quotes taken from *Holy Bible, New Living Translation,* Second Edition Copyright © 1996, 2004

Austin Brothers
Publishing

Books are available in quantity for promotional or educational use. Contact Austin Brothers Publishing for information at 3616 Sutter Ct., Fort Worth, TX 76137 or wterrya@gmail.com.

This and other books published by Austin Brothers Publishing can be purchased at www.abpbooks.com.

Printed in the United States of America

2016 -- First Edition

A special thanks to my wife Rita for her support in the creation of this book, and for being the mother of my five children.

Thanks to my father, Dr. A.R. Bernard, Senior Pastor of Christian Cultural Center, for all he has taught me and for his help in writing this book. Also, my mother, Karen Bernard, for always telling me that I could do whatever I put my mind to.

So we are Christ's ambassadors;
God is making his appeal through us.
We speak for Christ when we plead,
"Come back to God!"
(2 Corinthians 5:20)

Contents

Introduction

In 1959, the small island nation of Cuba off the Florida coast, experienced a revolution and the rise to power of Communist dictator Fidel Castro. Tension with the United States increased until finally, in 1961, the US severed all diplomatic ties and closed their embassy in Cuba. For decades there were no official conversations conducted between the two nations. Things changed in 2015 when the American Embassy was reopened, and the process of re-establishing a working relationship between the countries began.

When the US does not have an embassy and an ambassador in a country, communication and relationships are very difficult. The presence of an ambassador is extremely important. The ambassador is a direct representative of the President. He is chosen by the President, and speaks on behalf of the President to leaders of the foreign country. Consequently, the ambassador must be loyal to the President as well as a person who is well-respected by the leaders of the country where he works.

Whenever the President wants to establish a relationship with another country he sends an ambassador. Now read the words of the Apostle Paul describing the Christian's relationship to the world. In 2 Corinthians 5, he describes how our residency really belongs to another world, a world that is "eternal, in the heavens." Our dwelling on this earth is like living in a tent, which is a temporary residency. The fact that our real citizenship is in a much better place is a call to live in this world as representatives of that place. In other words, the spiritual part of our being is to take precedence over our physical world.

However, as long as we are in this world, we have an assignment. We are called to be ambassadors:

> *So we are Christ's ambassadors; God is making his appeal*
> *through us. We speak for Christ when we plead, "Come back*
> *to God!" (2 Corinthians 5:20)*

The same word translated "ambassador" in this instance was used by Jesus in two parables recorded in the Gospel of Luke (see Luke 14:32; 19:14). It was used by Jesus to describe a delegation or spokesperson for an owner or person in charge. They had the task of representing the interests of another, and to conduct business on their behalf.

Being an ambassador in the ancient world (Greek, Roman, or Jewish), especially because of the lack of communication and the inconvenience of travel, was an important position. Having someone serve as your ambassador was essential to doing business in a faraway place. The ambassador served two functions. First, they were a messenger. They carried the message that could not be communicated in any other manner.

The second function was to serve as a representative. This meant an ambassador was expected to carry out business and perform tasks on behalf of his master. When he spoke it was the same as the master speaking. When he made an agreement, he did so with full authority of the master. It was universally expected that an ambassador, whatever his message and however delicate or risky his mission, would be treated with respect and dignity. Historian and philosopher Philo spoke about a "law with regard to ambassadors," which indicated the diplomat represented the master and acted on his behalf and in his place, thus embodying his authority. To disregard or insult the envoy was to disregard or insult the sender.

In Luke 19, Jesus tells the story about the land owner who leased a vineyard. When his servants came to collect the rent, the tenants killed the servants on two different occasions. Finally, the landowner assumed they would respect his son, but they didn't, and he was also killed. The servants who were killed were acting as ambassadors for the landowner. They had the responsibility and authority to act on his behalf.

Having said all of that let me remind you again of Paul's words in 2 Corinthians:

So we are Christ's ambassadors; God is making his appeal through us. We speak for Christ when we plead, "Come back to God!" (2 Corinthians 5:20)

By establishing the church in the world, God opened up an embassy in order to relate to mankind. Now that Jesus has physically left (His entire excursion is the subject of many other books) we are now His ambassadors. As followers of Jesus, we have the responsibility to be His presence in the world.

The thesis of this book is that we are to be *Unapologetic Ambassadors for Christ*. This concept has become an important part of my ministry. I have observed, and experienced, how easy it is to apologize for our faith in Christ when confronted with a hostile world. Have you ever found yourself doing things like these?

- Remain silent when facing an opportunity to speak about your faith in Jesus.
- Snicker or laugh out loud when Christians are ridiculed and criticized.
- Filling your life with relationships and things that make it hard to live for Christ.
- Allowing distractions and worldly cares keep you from serving God.

If others don't know that you are a committed believer and follower of Jesus, it is likely that you are ashamed of being an ambassador for Christ.

I'm not talking about showing up at church two or three times a month. We are not just ambassadors for Christ when we gather for worship. It is more than raising our hands to the inspiring music, or shouting amen to the preached word. I'm talking about the life you live on Monday morning, Tuesday afternoon, Friday evening, and Saturday night. Are you living an unapologetic Christian life before your friends and family? Does the world know the hope that is in you because of Jesus Christ?

This life that I live is a life of conviction ...
A life that was gained from a life that was given
I'll tell the whole world even if they won't listen.

They can't shush me... I'm proud to be a Christian.

There is no separating.. my life from this walk
It's the way that I dress, how I think, how I talk
It is 365. It's 24-7
If you're offended I'm not sorry, for Christ I'm unapologetic

While they talk it. I live it
...Now a victor not victim.

The cross is my shield, He protects my decisions
My faith is made stronger. Fear is false evidence
Appearing real... They really think He isn't relevant
But what they don't see are the lives that He changed.
The joy that was gained from a life full of pain

I praise him. I live for him. I worship and lift my master up

A disciple. A son. A teacher. An ambassador. For Christ... Is
who I am. For Christ I am unashamed.

Before we can fully understand what it means to be an *Un-apologetic Ambassador for Christ*, it is imperative that we study the entire statement made by the Apostle Paul.

So we are Christ's ambassadors; God is making his appeal
through us. We speak for Christ when we plead, "Come back
to God!" (2 Corinthians 5:20)

Like the political ambassador of a country who goes with the authority of the President or King, the first thing we note is that we are sent out as ambassadors of Christ with God's authority. Paul says that "God is making his appeal through us."

I don't know about you, but it is extremely encouraging to me to know that I am not on my own. When we stand up and stand out for Christ, we are doing it under the authority of God. The authority of God! Run that through your mind several times. How can we be afraid to provide a witness for Christ to our friends when we speak with the authority of God? How can we sit by silently when people slander our faith when we have the opportunity to stand up in the authority of God?

Imagine how it would feel if the President of the United States asked you to represent him in a foreign country. He would provide instructions about what he wants, and then he might say, "Don't be afraid to speak up because you have my authority and the backing of the entire United States government standing with you."

If that were the case, can you imagine any scenario where you might cower in fear, afraid that you might be shunned? It would be highly unlikely that we would apologize for what we have been assigned to do.

But, do you realize that as an ambassador for Christ, we do not have the power and influence of the President of the United States, or any other world leader—we speak and act under the authority of God. The creator, sustainer, and ruler of the universe is the one who has sent us out as His ambassadors.

Not only do we have the authority of God as His ambassadors, but we are also equipped with His message. The word Paul uses is translated "appeal" and comes from a compound Greek word that literally means "call to" or God is calling people to Himself through us. As ambassadors, we hold the message of calling others to God. It is a dynamic message that God wants people to come to Him, a message that is empowered by God Himself, through us, His ambassadors. This is an amazing image.

A third thing we note in this verse is that we are speaking "for Christ." Don Miller is a well-known writer and speaker, especially popular among young Christians. He relates an experience he had while teaching a class in Canada. His students were all freshman college students who had grown up in the church. The class was called "The Gospel and Culture," and he began with an experiment.

Miller instructed the class that he was going to share the gospel of Jesus, but was going to leave something out. Their task was to listen to his presentation and identify what part of the Gospel he had omitted.

He spoke about sin, and how we are all fallen creatures. He told stories and provided graphic illustrations that resonated with the students. He talked about repentance, again using stories and illustrations. From there he moved on to speak of God's forgiveness, before he concluded with an explanation of heaven and what to expect when you are saved.

After a twenty minute presentation of the Gospel, he then asked the class to identify what he had omitted from the discussion. There was a lot of silence and mumbling, but not one student had realized he had left Jesus out of his presentation of the Gospel. Not one student!

The same thing happens frequently with many of us. We talk about church, even sharing our testimony of God's goodness and the blessings He provides in our lives. That is all good. We might even feel especially brave and speak of sin, and the need for forgiveness.

However, until we relay the message of Jesus and what He has done on our behalf, we have not presented the Gospel. We are ambassadors for Christ, not the good life, or the road to blessings, or the ticket to heaven. The heart of the gospel, the heart of the message of reconciliation, is the death and resurrection of Jesus Christ. Our message is Jesus Christ. As ambassadors, we are to speak for Him.

The final aspect we will note of Paul's statement concerns the goal, or more accurately the hope of mankind, and that is the call to "come back to God." Perhaps a better translation of the term is "to be reconciled."

Think back to the story about the American Embassy reopening in Cuba. When Pope Francis visited Cuba he called attention to the relationship between the two countries, the United States and Cuba. At the time it was a politically charged environment, and he called upon the countries to "set an example of reconciliation" for the rest of the world. When these two nations, which had been at odds with each other for decades, came together, it was a reconciliation.

That is exactly why God has sent us into the world—to provide an opportunity of reconciliation. His desire is to be in relationship with all men, but not all men know or understand this is what God wants.

People have all kinds of ideas about God. You encounter them every day. Some think He is like a kind old white-haired grandfather handing out gifts to His grandchildren. Others see Him as a benevolent dictator, ruling the world with a kind heart.

Still others have the equally mistaken notion that God is angry, wishing to reveal His wrath on those who get out of line. Perhaps one of the most common misunderstandings is the idea that God simply set the world in motion and then disappeared to let it run by itself.

The truth is found in the message His ambassadors bring to the world—God wants to live in relationship with us.

Our family always prays before we eat a meal together. I enjoy the fact that my kids like this idea so much that they fight over who is going to pray. These are the habits that we as Christians should have that are consistent with our lifestyle. We will take a look at lifestyle and culture later in the book.

At a restaurant one Sunday, after we prayed, I felt people from a nearby table look at me in contempt. It bothered me, not because they stared at me, but the fact that they had a problem with me expressing my faith. Often in our society, the actions and words of many are considered acceptable as they express their beliefs or ideology, but let a Christian say or do something, and it is unacceptable. I'm discouraged from saying the name "Jesus" in a public forum, school, or on television because there needs to be sensitivity to others.

This is where I was provoked to start the campaign of "don't shush me." I feel that my Christianity is a significant part of my lifestyle, and it is not something that can be silenced. To tell me to be quiet is to tell not to live. When I accepted Jesus into my life I was reborn into a lifestyle called Christianity.

My Christianity does not have an on and off switch, nor does it have some type of dimmer switch. I cannot separate myself from my Christianity no more than my wife can separate herself from being Puerto Rican. Even though she is living in America she is still considered Spanish. Just like I am Black. When I eat, sleep, walk, work, play, live, or die I am Black. So the same goes for my Christianity. I am Christian when I am eating, sleeping, walking, working, playing, living, or dying.

I can truly say that I was born this way, and this is not something you can shush. If people can say and do what they want, even if it makes me feel uncomfortable, then why can't we as Christians do the same? As social norms change what is accepted by society changes, then we as the church need to be the moral compass for this world. At one time it was wrong to say any type of curse word on TV but now things have changed. If the voice of the church does not hold the culture accountable things will continue to progress for the worse.

Unapologetic Ambassadors for Christ (UAFC) is a movement. This movement began as a discussion with my father, Pastor A. R. Bernard Sr. We were talking about my feelings on how we as Christians needed to walk a life that will not allow people to "shush" us. As we brainstormed, we first came up with the concept of "Don't Shush Me." Momentum was created; we got the team involved in the brainstorming process, and we started "Don't Shush Me." Concepts were created, websites were being discussed, and materials produced.

I called my father to give him an update, and he asked me where I wanted to go with this concept? I explained my desire was to empower people to walk in boldness, like Peter and John in the days of the early church. He then suggested that the name "Don't Shush Me" wouldn't go far because that statement has limitations.

I remember that night like it was yesterday. I was annoyed, because I felt like I was wasting time, and could possibly lose momentum. I must say that I was not the nicest person on the phone with my father that night. (Side note; this is why I love the relationship my father and I have. He allows me to grow to the things that he is trying to teach me).

As we spoke on the phone he said "The idea that you are trying to convey is that people must be Unapologetic."

I recognized it immediately and replied, "That's correct, unapologetic about the apologetics. ("Apologetics" is a term used by theologians to describe defending the faith.)

Then he asked, "For who?"

And I said, "For Christ."

This is what brought about the birth of UAFC. *Unapologetic Ambassadors for Christ* is a movement designed to encourage people to enter an authentic relationship with Christ. Also, to encourage Christians to be emboldened with a desire to live out their Christianity unapologetically, never being ashamed of the gospel. The movement will also seek to become a voice in areas where I feel the church has been quiet, or has been slow to move; areas such as anti bullying, anti human sex trafficking, religious freedom, anti violence, and others. My hope is that UAFC will spread contagiously through other churches and non-profit agencies.

The movement of UAFC will push Christians to worship God and preach the gospel within a certain lifestyle. This lifestyle is one that is consistent with the word of God. It will be governed by a conviction that is designed specifically for that individual.

John McArthur states that there are two major contributors to the powerlessness of the church. One is ignorance of Biblical truth, and the other is that in spite of knowledge of biblical truth we fail to live up to it. The plan is to develop workshops, conferences, mission trips, and services that will equip people to overcome these two obstacles.

When a person receives Christ, they should represent Christ in culture all day every day. Do you begin to understand why we must not be apologetic about our faith? God and the world both need us to be *Unapologetic Ambassadors for Christ*. What an amazing assignment we have been given. What an incredible opportunity stands before us.

I invite you to read through the pages of this book and learn more about what it means to approach our role as ambassadors with courage, confidence, and conviction.

Section 1

The Christians' Role in the World

Representing God's Culture

In 1963, there was a television show called, *My Favorite Martian*. The premise of the show was that a one-man Martian space ship crash-landed on earth. The lone Martian lived on earth, incognito, as he attempted to repair his space ship. That was followed by another show in 1978 that introduced us to Robin Williams as an alien visitor to earth in the show *Mork and Mindy*. In 1996 we met the lovable family of aliens living together in the show, *Third Rock from the Sun*.

Along the way we have also met aliens from other planets, such as *E.T.* and the *Men in Black* series, all featuring aliens from outer space who are striving to live unrecognized on planet earth. Sometimes they have been scary, but more often they come across funny as they strive to adapt to our unusual ways and customs.

It is likely that you have traveled to a foreign country and been exposed to a world with different customs and values. It takes some time to adapt when all those around us have different habits and language. But, it usually doesn't take long being immersed in a foreign culture until we begin to feel at home. Such is not the case if you were from an entirely different world.

Similarly, Christians represent an entirely different world than the place they live. As ambassadors of Christ, we have been placed in this world to represent the world of the One who sent us—Jesus Christ.

There is an old Gospel song that you might remember, *This World is Not My Home.*

> *This world is not my home I'm just a-passin' through*
> *My treasures are laid up somewhere beyond the blue.*
> *The angels beckon me from heaven's open door*
> *And I can't feel at home in this world anymore.*

> *Oh Lord, You know I have no friend like you*
> *If heaven's not my home then Lord what will I do?*
> *The angels beckon me from heaven's open door*
> *And I can't feel at home in this world anymore.*

Although our feet are firmly planted on the soil of planet earth, this is not our home. It has been said, "we are in the world, but not of the world." One of the tasks of an ambassador is to represent his culture to the world where He now resides. As we will see in our study of scripture, this means the Christian is a representative of a heavenly world to those in a worldly environment.

The 17th chapter of the Gospel of John contains the words of Jesus as He prayed for His disciples. It is Jesus speaking to His Father on behalf of His followers. The overriding concept through the entire prayer is Jesus' great love for His disciples.

His prayer shows great concern that they are about to be set loose in a hostile world.

It is important to note that Jesus does not pray that His followers will be removed from the world, or even be elevated above the world. He does not ask that they will be exempt from the struggles and pain of the world. Instead, He clearly recognizes that even though they are not "of the world" they are nevertheless "in the world."

> *I'm not asking you to take them out of the world, but to keep them safe from the evil one. They do not belong to this world any more than I do. (Matthew 17:15-16)*

That is also a clear expression of the life of an ambassador. They live in a country, but they are not of that country. As ambassadors of Christ, we live in this world, but we are not of this world. Therefore, the basic issue of being a good ambassador is to understand, and be able to represent their culture to the foreign culture where they live.

Jesus repeatedly warns in His prayer recorded in John 17 that the culture of His followers is much different than the culture of the world. Ever since He uttered that prayer, Christians have been striving to understand the difference between the two worlds. If we are going to be *Unapologetic Ambassadors for Christ*, we must understand what it means to live according to the culture of Christ.

I want to explain it to you by using a term that is not used often by followers of Jesus, but it is a powerful word used frequently in scripture. It is the word "holy." We are to live "holy" lives. To be holy simply means to be separated. To be holy is to be separated from the secular and given to God. The consequence of this separation is a distinct difference in our lives. Our goal as Ambassadors for Christ is holiness. To become holy is to be separated from the world and filled with God. This is our world, our culture.

In describing a holy life there are two things that must be meticulously avoided. The first is the tendency to define the Christian life in negative terms. The tendency is to say, "A holy person does not drink, dance, cuss, or gamble or associate with those who do." The problem is that we can avoid all of these things and still be worldly.

The New Testament Pharisees, literally known as the "separate ones," understood holiness in negative terms. They developed the concept of a fence around the law to insure law keeping. What that means is that they avoided unnecessary things lest they get too close to doing the forbidden things. Perhaps your grandparents talked about drinking alcohol because it leads to drunkenness, or holding hands because it leads to sex.

William Coleman in a cleverly titled book, *Pharisees Guide to Total Holiness* said, "If we dance, who knows where it might lead? Back up two steps and build a fence. Some movies could corrupt—two more steps back and build another fence. Who knows where wine at mealtime might lead? More fence. Eventually we are no longer wrestling with the core problems of drunkenness and adultery. Rather we are fighting mock battles at the new fences we have erected. Now the new laws become the really important battlegrounds. Soon we will test a person's orthodoxy by his respect for the fences."

Such prohibition of activities promotes legalism. We must not define holiness in these terms. If holiness only involves keeping a set of rules, anyone could achieve it in their own strength. Again the Pharisees provide an example. They kept thousands of rules; yet note Jesus' estimation of the Pharisees.

What sorrow awaits you teachers of religious law and you Pharisees. Hypocrites! For you are like whitewashed tombs— beautiful on the outside but filled on the inside with dead people's bones and all sorts of impurity. Outwardly you look like righteous people, but inwardly your hearts are filled with hypocrisy and lawlessness. (Matthew. 23:27-28)

Holiness is separation, but we are mistaken if we concentrate merely on the external. Of primary importance is inner separation. If we are separated from the world inwardly then the outward will take care of itself.

Holiness will be expressed in a Christian lifestyle. It is accomplished by allowing the Holy Spirit within to express Himself outwardly. What I am talking about here is the way to live a life that will allow us to be unapologetic in our witness for Christ.

So think clearly and exercise self-control. Look forward to the gracious salvation that will come to you when Jesus Christ is revealed to the world. So you must live as God's obedient children. Don't slip back into your old ways of living to satisfy your own desires. You didn't know any better then. But now you must be holy in everything you do, just as God who chose you is holy. For the Scriptures say, "You must be holy because I am holy." (1 Peter 1:13-17)

Peter begins with an illustration of holiness and how it is like an obedient child. The basic meaning of the word translated "obedient" means "to hear." When a child is slow to obey, a parent will often say, "Did you hear me?"

The Apostle Paul reminds us that all of us are slaves, either to Satan or God, either to sin or righteousness (Romans 6:16). Who you obey is your master. If your obedience is to sin, then the result is death. If your obedience is to God, the result is righteousness.

We are God's children, which defines an intimate relationship we have with God. As children have a desire to imitate their parents, we should imitate our heavenly Father, the Holy One. Thus, as obedient children, we become holy. The supreme example is Jesus (see Philippians 2:8). What does an obedient child look like? Look at Jesus. He demonstrated holiness in every situation. Do what Jesus did! He is our example of holiness.

The same call to holiness is found in Romans 12:1-2:

> *And so, dear brothers and sisters, I plead with you to give your bodies to God because of all he has done for you. Let them be a living and holy sacrifice—the kind he will find acceptable. This is truly the way to worship him. Don't copy the behavior and customs of this world, but let God transform you into a new person by changing the way you think. Then you will learn to know God's will for you, which is good and pleasing and perfect.*

We are admonished in our quest for holiness to not "copy the behavior and customs of this world." If holiness is separation from the world then it must be non-conformity to the world. "Conform" means to pour into a mold, to assume the outward appearance but not necessarily representative of the inner. The pattern or mold of conformity is "behavior and customs of this world." If our desires are wealth, success, fame, power, and the other things the world seeks, then our life will conform to these ideals. We must not be conformed. The world desires one thing, the Christian another.

The problem is "ignorance" which means without knowledge. The reason Christians conform to the world is ignorance. If the Bible is God's Word and true, then to conform to another standard is ignorant. It is sad to see among Christians:

No money to give, spent on the world

No time to worship, invested in the world

No energy to serve, expended in the world

Many years ago, Ray Kroc, founder and president of McDonalds was asked about the beliefs that motive him to success. He replied, "God, my family and McDonald's hamburgers, and when I get to the office I reverse the order." Many Christians would substitute something else for McDonalds but the idea would be tragically the same. We are admonished to not be like the world.

Returning to the words of Peter, we notice that he says, "... you must be holy." The word "be" is not from "being" but from "becoming." Thus it describes "becoming holy." It is a process, not happening instantly. We look at ourselves and see unholiness, worldliness. Remember, we are "becoming holy." We are in a process. One of the evidences of genuine salvation is "am I becoming holy?" Are you more like Jesus today than you were yesterday? (see Philippians 1:6)

We are to be holy "in all your behavior..." This includes everything we do. No area of life is exempt. Impurity in one area of life will drag us down in every area of life. Holiness must encompass everything about us. Holiness within will be expressed through a Christian lifestyle.

For centuries, men have tried to win the battle by keeping the law, and it continues today with legalists building an elaborate system of right and wrong. The problem is that the law is unable to produce holiness within us.

Let me explain what happens and you think about whether this resonates with your own experience. You go to church on Sunday and listen to the sermon about living a pure life or avoiding a specific sin. You fall under conviction because you know your own failure. So you make a promise to God and yourself that you will get it right. You set out on Monday morning to live for Jesus and be the person God wants you to be. How long does that last for you? About as long as a New Year's resolution or a diet. When someone brings up the idea of living for Jesus or being holy and we say, "I tried, but..."

Consequently, we become "Apologetic" Ambassadors for Christ. Our behavior is not consistent with the Christ we represent. It would be like the new US Ambassador to Cuba living in such a way that no one realizes he represents the President.

The moon has no light on its own, it merely reflects the sun. That reflection changes throughout each month so we see a full moon that gradually changes into a crescent moon. That is the way it is with holiness. We have no holiness ourselves but we can reflect Jesus. The more we reflect Him the brighter our light.

The question now becomes, how do we reflect Jesus? That is the focus of the remainder of this book.

Sometimes we get carried away and eat so much candy that we lose hunger for nutritious food. In a similar manner, we can consume so much of the world that we lose our hunger for the spiritual things of God. What we need is a spiritual diet rather than filling up on the things of the world. It is like eating junk food which ruins your health, especially spiritual health. The prerequisite for holiness is separation. Only then will you hunger for holiness.

Reflections:

To be "holy" means to live separate from the things of the world. What are the things of the world that are most difficult for you to give up?

Describe a time when you knew that you were controlled (led) by the Holy Spirit. How did it affect your actions?

What are some things you can do that will make your reflection of Jesus brighter?

Speaking on Behalf of Another

You have probably heard of the term "power of attorney." In fact, it is likely that you have been given the power of attorney on behalf or an ailing parent or other relative. It allows you to speak on their behalf simply because they are no longer able to represent or speak for themselves. It is most often seen as people get older and lose some of their mental or physical capacities.

If you are a responsible person and are given the power of attorney for someone else, no doubt you want to make decisions according to their will and interests. For example, you wouldn't want to give their money away to strangers unless you knew that is what they wanted. Also, you would not allow them to be kept alive artificially unless you knew that was their wish.

An ambassador does not have the power of attorney for the president, but he does have the responsibility to speak on behalf of the president. In fact, that is one of his primary responsibilities—to explain and interpret the desires of the one he represents.

As ambassadors for Christ we have the responsibility, and opportunity, to speak on behalf of Christ. This is an awesome duty, requiring several things in order for us to carry about the task effectively.

Speaking on behalf of Christ is a frequent theme in the Bible. Since the written word of God was completed years ago, the spread of the Gospel has been dependent upon the spoken word from God's people. I'm not just talking about the preaching that takes place by those standing in the pulpit on Sunday morning, but also the words spoken by God's people as they live their lives as His ambassadors.

> *...but sanctify Christ as Lord in your hearts, always being ready to make a defense to everyone who asks you to give an account for the hope that is in you, yet with gentleness and reverence; (1 Peter 3:15)*

Instead, you must worship Christ as Lord of your life. And if someone asks about your Christian hope, always be ready to explain it. But do this in a gentle and respectful way.

The context of these words is a word of encouragement from Peter to Christians who are facing persecution for their faith. The early Christians had to live out their faith in a hostile world, one much more hostile to Christianity than anything you and I will experience from our culture. Peter admonishes them to continue to do good as a means of avoiding harm, but then adds, "But even if you suffer for doing what is right, God will reward you for it" (1 Peter 3:14).

In other words, even after doing good things, don't be surprised if you encounter those who want to stop you from following Christ, those who find you offensive. Instead of being afraid of their threats and accusations, we are to continue to speak out on behalf of Christ.

In your world, you might be embarrassed at times to speak up for Christ. You might be afraid to call attention to Jesus because you don't want to be labeled, and considered some kind of a fanatic. Apparently, if that is your situation, you would have fit in perfectly well with the people of the first century who belonged to the church.

An ambassador cannot fulfill his duties by remaining silent. There comes a time when he must explain and defend the decisions and actions of his own country. It is the duty of an ambassador to speak on behalf of his own nation.

That is exactly what Peter is saying to followers of Jesus when he says, "always be ready to explain" the Christian hope. As we dig deeper into this verse we will notice four important things that can equip us to be *Unapologetic Ambassadors for Christ*.

Preparation for speaking comes from making Christ the Lord of your life.

The single most important characteristic of an unapologetic ambassador for Christ is one who has made Jesus Christ the Lord of their life. Once again we have uncovered a subject that is worthy of an entire book (or several volumes of books). What does it mean to have Jesus as Lord of your life?

The phrase literally reads, "Sanctify God as lord in your heart." The term "sanctify" means "to set apart" and is the same word that is often translated as "holy." Essentially what Peter is saying is that we are to set God apart from everything in our lives so that He is Lord.

Rather than being afraid to speak up and fulfill your task as an ambassador, an unapologetic ambassador honors Christ as holy. He is our king, the master of our domain. We are not here to serve anyone or anything else. All of our praise and honor belong to Him. Do you understand how this will fill you with power? Once you recognize that Jesus is the One to be worshipped, the One who is holy, you will no longer be intimidated by others.

The battle belongs to the Lord. We are simply His spokesperson. This is what happens when we recognize His greatness instead of obsessing over the opinions and actions of others. When we arrive at this point we will have great power to speak on His behalf.

However, if you have not allowed Christ to be Lord of your life, you have put yourself in the position of responding to the call of someone else. In other words, you have become an ambassador for another. Preparation for being an *Unapologetic Ambassador for Christ* is to "worship Christ as Lord of your life."

The recipients of our speech are the ones who notice how we live.

As *Unapologetic Ambassadors for Christ*, our speech is to be directed to those who ask about the hope that is within us. What Peter is saying is that if we live under the lordship of Jesus Christ, people will want to know what is different about us. Let me see if I can explain what this means.

When you go through a tragedy, say for example the death of a loved one, your friends and neighbors will observe your response. They will examine your grief, and they will be aware of your hurt from the loss. However, if they see you standing firm in your faith in God through the experience, and they are aware that your loss only strengthened your hope in God, they will ask. They will want to know how it is possible.

I can speak from my personal experience with the death of my brother. When my brother died he was just 39 years old. He was getting his health together, he had lost 30 pounds, and in the midst of all the good things. He died from a bad asthma attack. God was good, and I was able to stand firm in my faith. Consequently, I was able to minister to people without even speaking. I realized that people were watching, they wanted to see if my faith was real.

Or, perhaps, they will hear that you have lost a job, or suffered some type of financial setback, perhaps your car is stolen or your house burns down, they will notice if you fall apart or if you remain resolved in your faith. They will want to know how it is possible.

Or, perhaps when a young adult says no to negative peer pressure and avoids places and activities that are harmful, it might take awhile, but the day will come when your friends notice a difference in your life. They will see that you have maintained your steadfastness in Christ. They will want to know how it is possible.

Or, as a parent of older children, people will see how you handle the loss of a child, or the failures of your children. They will notice that you didn't fall apart when your child suffered, and that you didn't wander around in desperation or get lost in the fog of anger when your child made major mistakes. They will see that you weathered the storm and found hope. They will want to know how it is possible.

When they come to you and ask about your hope that is when you become the most powerful ambassador for Christ. At that point you have no reason for apology. There will be no reason for embarrassment or fear. You can listen to their questions and proudly point them to Jesus, the One you serve and the One you represent.

Remember, Peter was speaking to early Christians who were required to stand before a judge or tribunal and answer about their faith in Christ, often with their life at stake. If they were expected to be unapologetic about Christ at that point, how can we be reluctant when confronted by an inquisitive friend or curious neighbor? If Jesus is Lord of our life, we will not hide from opportunities to speak His name at appropriate times.

One day, Jesus encountered a man who was so demon possessed that his nickname was "Legion" because of the number of demons in his life (see Mark 5). He was violent and uncontrollable, frightening to everyone who came near him. Jesus cast the demons out of the man and into a nearby heard of swine where they met their destruction. The result was a new man, one who was now civilized and in full control of his faculties.

As you can imagine, the man wanted to stay with Jesus, to travel with Him and his disciples around the countryside. However, Jesus sent him away with these words: "No, go home to your family, and tell them everything the Lord has done for you and how merciful he has been" (Mark 5:19).

Why did Jesus send him home to his family and friends? Because they are the ones who would most clearly see the difference in the man. You've heard testimonies from people who speak about how miserable their life was at one point but they found Jesus. Sometimes, over the years of telling and retelling the story, their life before Jesus gets worse and worse (perhaps a little "ministerial exaggeration").

However, those who know us best are the ones who most easily and clearly recognize the hope that Christ has instilled within us. They see the change. And when they ask us about what is different that is when we must speak up most enthusiastically as *Unapologetic Ambassadors for Christ.*

The content of our speech is our hope in Christ.

When Peter speaks about the hope within us it is a reference to the Christian faith. It is simply another way of identifying what you believe. It is to be able to provide a rational explanation and reasoned defense for why we are believers and followers of Christ.

There are two things that hurt the church: 1) a lack of biblical teaching, and 2) and lack of living it out. The lack of knowledge among believers is especially troublesome today. In a sense, the church has been guilty of "dumbing down" the truth to make it more appealing to the masses. Many churches are so concerned with drawing crowds that they have been unwilling to ask believers to pay the price to learn the Word of God. Many sermons are little more than "feel-good" homilies designed not to offend or discourage.

The reality is that the Word of God is powerful (see Hebrews 4:12), and if we avail ourselves of good, solid, biblical teaching our lives with be filled with power. Perhaps one of the main reasons followers of Christ are not consistently living according to the Christian faith is because they have not learned the Word of God.

When people ask about the hope that is within us, all we have to offer that makes any difference is the truth about our faith in Christ. If an ambassador in a foreign country did not have communication from his own government, he would have nothing to say, no reason to speak, no reason to even exist. We will not be able to answer everything about Christ (and people will ask you questions you can't answer), but God gives us what He wants us to know. Be secure that Christ died for you, interceding on your behalf. That security will preach further than anything else.

Peter is simply asking us to be able to defend our Christianity. Be prepared to tell people why you believe what you believe. It is crucial to understand why you believe what you believe, and then be able to share it with those who ask.

The manner of our speech is to be gentle and respectful.

The word "gentleness" is actually the word for meekness or humility. The word is often mistaken for the idea of weakness or without strength. The reality is that it describes power under control. The word was sometimes used to describe a wild horse that had been tamed. It was just as strong, but now it is under control.

The other term used by Peter is "respectful," or more correctly understood as "reverence." This Greek term is the word *phobou*. You know about "phobias." That is the same word used here to describe our speech. We are to speak with the kind of reverence that stems from fear. Now when Scripture speaks of fearing God it is not to be understood as fear that God will harm us if we do something wrong. Quite the contrary, God has gone out of His way to rescue us from the consequence of our sin. This attitude of reverence arises from truly understanding who God is in relation to who we are.

Listen to the words of the Old Testament prophet Isaiah:

It was in the year King Uzziah died that I saw the Lord. He was sitting on a lofty throne, and the train of his robe filled the Temple. Attending him were mighty seraphim, each having six wings. With two wings they covered their faces, with two they covered their feet, and with two they flew.

They were calling out to each other,
"Holy, holy, holy is the LORD of Heaven's Armies!
The whole earth is filled with his glory!"

Their voices shook the Temple to its foundations, and the entire building was filled with smoke.

Then I said, "It's all over! I am doomed, for I am a sinful man. I have filthy lips, and I live among a people with filthy lips. Yet I have seen the King, the LORD of Heaven's Armies."

Then one of the seraphim flew to me with a burning coal he had taken from the altar with a pair of tongs. He touched my lips with it and said, "See, this coal has touched your lips. Now your guilt is removed, and your sins are forgiven."

Then I heard the Lord asking, "Whom should I send as a messenger to this people? Who will go for us?" I said, "Here I am. Send me."

And he said, "Yes, go, and say to this people... (Isaiah 6:1-9)

When you combine these two terms as a description of the way we testify on behalf of Christ, they suggest we speak with strength and confidence, not overpowering, but with convincing and convicting power. When an ambassador for Christ speaks, people will take note.

The great English preacher from days long ago, Charles Spurgeon said, "It seems to me that the chief business of a Christian while here below is to speak on God's behalf."

That is why we are here. That is who we are—*Unapologetic Ambassadors for Christ.*

But you will receive power when the Holy Spirit comes upon you. And you will be my witnesses, telling people about me everywhere—in Jerusalem, throughout Judea, in Samaria, and to the ends of the earth. (Acts 1:8)

Reflections:

Describe a recent experience when you were embarrassed or too afraid to speak on behalf of Jesus.

What are some actions that your friends see in your life that suggest you are a believer?

What are some things about Jesus that you could say to your non-believing friends that would not be offensive or push them away?

Skilled Tactician

In one of his most important positions, Benjamin Franklin was the American ambassador to France at a critical time in American history—the American Revolution. He was highly respected and admired by the French people, and members of French high society. Some have said he most clearly fits the definition of a Renaissance man because of his numerous interests, attributes, and accomplishments.

Ambassador Franklin's efforts to gain the support of the French on behalf of the Americans were essential for securing military aid to the struggling colonies. France signed a military alliance with the emerging colonies in 1778, only two years after the revolution began. He also negotiated the Treaty of Paris in 1783, which formally ended the American war for Independence.

Many historians have concluded that Benjamin Franklin was the only person who could have accomplished what many in the colonies thought was an impossible feat. John Adams, who later became the second President of the US was also assigned to assist Franklin in his mission as an ambassador to France, but the French found Adams so distasteful that he was almost completely ignored, and had to return home.

It is important for an ambassador to be a skilled tactician. As we learn from Benjamin Franklin, an ambassador might be the difference between significant victory and devastating defeat.

As ambassadors for Christ, it is equally important that we develop the skills necessary to be effective. If you intend to be an *Unapologetic Ambassador for Christ* you will need some tactical skills to make it possible.

A carpenter needs skills in handling wood and tools, and a mechanic needs to understand engines and how they work. A Wall Street banker must be skilled in the ways of investments, just as a nurse must understand the tools of the medical field. In the same way, an ambassador for Christ must be a skilled tactician. If we are lacking in skills, we might actually do harm for the cause of Christ.

There are three tools that are essential for an unapologetic ambassador for Christ. Possessing these tools will equip you for success in sharing the hope that is within you through Jesus Christ.

The first tool is knowledge; having an accurate mind.

Work hard so you can present yourself to God and receive his approval. Be a good worker, one who does not need to be ashamed and who correctly explains the word of truth. (2 Timothy 2:15)

In the words of the Apostle Paul to the young preacher Timothy, we read the admonition to work hard at handling the Word of God. We are to be diligent in the task of learning the Word of God. The first skill we must develop as ambassadors for Christ is to know and understand the scriptures.

People are going to ask questions about your faith. They will ask some very difficult questions about faith; questions that theologians have debated for centuries. However, you have a responsibility to learn and prepare to answer them as best you can. I'm not saying you have to be a seminary trained theologian to be an ambassador for Christ, but I am saying there is no excuse for failing to learn more and more every day.

The Bible should be your close friend and constant companion. You should read it and study it every day. Look again at Paul's words to Timothy—we should be one who "does not need to be ashamed." He is picking up the same idea we have been discussing that we must be *Unapologetic Ambassadors for Christ*.

The minimum requirement for an ambassador is to know the character, mind, and purposes of his king. The ambassador is taking the message of the sovereign, on behalf of the sovereign, to the people of another nation. Communication between the ambassador and the king are crucial. All of the American embassies have direct lines of communication that are frequently utilized to make sure the proper message gets to the proper place.

It is important that we have clear and open communication with Christ if we are to be a faithful ambassador in His service. I'm speaking of Bible study—the way He speaks to us, and prayer—the way we speak to Him.

Knowledge is an indispensable skill for the ambassador. Our words and message do not have to be clever, but they do have to be accurate and clear. You will be pleasantly surprised at how much bolder you will feel and act when you know what you believe and why you believe it. You will have courage and confidence to live out your faith.

The second tool is wisdom; knowing when and how to apply knowledge.

Joyful is the person who finds wisdom,
the one who gains understanding.
For wisdom is more profitable than silver,
and her wages are better than gold.
Wisdom is more precious than rubies;
nothing you desire can compare with her.
She offers you long life in her right hand,
and riches and honor in her left.
She will guide you down delightful paths;
all her ways are satisfying.
Wisdom is a tree of life to those who embrace her; happy are
those who hold her tightly. (Proverbs 3:13-18)

Wisdom is closely related to knowledge, but they are not the same thing. Some have defined wisdom as "artful knowledge." It is the ability to utilize and deploy knowledge in the appropriate time and manner. Knowledge is having information, but wisdom is the ability to properly utilize that information.

As Christians, it is imperative that we are informed about our faith, but in order to be successful ambassadors we must know how to share that information. Tactful, artful diplomacy makes our message persuasive. Wisdom is the ability to know what to say, when to say it, and how to say it. It is the ability to judge correctly and follow the best course of action.

Wisdom comes from God.

If you need wisdom, ask our generous God, and he will give it to you. He will not rebuke you for asking. (James 1:5)

In the Old Testament, Solomon prayed for wisdom. When you read his biography it is obvious he did always employ wisdom, but there were times when his wisdom produced amazing results. One such incident is recorded in 1 Kings.

Sometime later two prostitutes came to the king to have an argument settled.

"Please, my lord," one of them began, "this woman and I live in the same house. I gave birth to a baby while she was with me in the house. Three days later this woman also had a baby. We were alone; there were only two of us in the house.

"But her baby died during the night when she rolled over on it. Then she got up in the night and took my son from beside me while I was asleep. She laid her dead child in my arms and took mine to sleep beside her. And in the morning when I tried to nurse my son, he was dead! But when I looked more closely in the morning light, I saw that it wasn't my son at all."

Then the other woman interrupted, "It certainly was your son, and the living child is mine."

"No," the first woman said, "the living child is mine, and the dead one is yours."

And so they argued back and forth before the king. Then the king said, "Let's get the facts straight. Both of you claim the living child is yours, and each says that the dead one belongs to the other. All right, bring me a sword."

So a sword was brought to the king. Then he said, "Cut the living child in two, and give half to one woman and half to the other!"

Then the woman who was the real mother of the living child, and who loved him very much, cried out, "Oh no, my lord! Give her the child—please do not kill him!"

But the other woman said, "All right, he will be neither yours nor mine; divide him between us!"

Then the king said, "Do not kill the child, but give him to the woman who wants him to live, for she is his mother!"

When all Israel heard the king's decision, the people were in awe of the king, for they saw the wisdom God had given him for rendering justice. (1 Kings 3:16-28)

Solomon had the basic knowledge that a real mother would care so deeply about her child that she would do anything to protect the baby. However, it took wisdom to know how to apply that knowledge and uncover the truth. This is also a trait we need in order to be *Unapologetic Ambassadors for Christ*.

The third tool is character; a manner that is attractive to others.

An ambassador brings himself into every situation and in everything he does and says, so personal maturity and individual virtue can either make or break the message. Ralph Waldo Emerson once said, "Who you are speaks so loudly I can't hear what you're saying."

> *If I could speak all the languages of earth and of angels, but didn't love others, I would only be a noisy gong or a clanging cymbal. If I had the gift of prophecy, and if I understood all of God's secret plans and possessed all knowledge, and if I had such faith that I could move mountains, but didn't love others, I would be nothing. (1 Corinthians 13:1-2)*

Your friends and family will not listen to what you have to say about your faith if you are obnoxious and unlikable. Others will not be interested in hearing your testimony if you come across as dishonest and uncaring.

An extremely valuable tool in the ambassador's toolbox is character—the kind of character that attracts and inspires others. Many politicians have been elected, not necessarily because of their great ideas and plans, but because people liked and trusted them. Many people have succeeded in business, not because of their great vision and inspirational speeches, but because of their attractive character.

We need to make sure that we are more than a "noisy gong or a clanging cymbal" to those who need to hear our message. Character not only allows us to have a hearing, but also gives authenticity to our message. Simply put, when people see the reality in our lives they will believe the words from our lips. Then we truly become *Unapologetic Ambassadors for Christ*.

Have you ever been out somewhere and have your car breakdown because of something that should be a simple fix, but you didn't have the proper tool? Or, perhaps you are trying to make something special in the kitchen, and no matter how hard you search through the pantry, an essential ingredient is missing? Or, maybe you are trying to finish up a project at work and an important file is not on your computer? If so, you know how easy it is to waste a lot of time and effort trying to make do without an essential tool. In fact, it often is the difference between succeeding and failing.

To be an *Unapologetic Ambassador for Christ* we must have all the necessary tools. It is not enough to be a believer; we must also know what we believe and why we believe it. It is necessary to be wise enough to use this information in the proper way, and at the right time. In addition, if our character is lacking, we will not be heard. Becoming skillful with the tools of Christ's ambassador is a lifetime task, and I invite you to join me in the journey.

Reflections:

How much time do you spend each week learning how to handle God's Word?

What skills do you need to be a better spokesperson for Jesus?

Is there anything about your life that will undermine your speech about your faith in God?

Avoiding Failure

When most people get a new job, it takes some time, at least a few weeks or even a few months, before they begin making an impact. When it comes to politics we hear a lot of talk about the "first one hundred days" for a new President of the United States and the importance of establishing an early presence. However, it's almost unheard of that someone would make a significant impact the first day on the job.

Such is not the case with the Apostle Peter and his first day on the job as an ambassador for Christ. He and the other disciples were instructed by Jesus to wait for their assignment. They gathered in the Upper Room, praying and waiting for whatever God had for them. They had been told they would take the message to the world (see Acts 1:8), but it was not yet time. They were to wait.

Finally, on the Day of Pentecost, the Holy Spirit showed up, and they were given the assignment. The first day on the job as an ambassador for Christ saw Peter standing before the crowd and preaching Jesus. He preached a marvelous sermon about the history of God and the salvation offered through Jesus. When he finished, listen to what happened:

> *Peter's words pierced their hearts, and they said to him and to the other apostles, "Brothers, what should we do?"*
>
> *Peter replied, "Each of you must repent of your sins, turn to God, and be baptized in the name of Jesus Christ to show that you have received forgiveness for your sins. Then you will receive the gift of the Holy Spirit. This promise is to you, and to your children, and even to the Gentiles—all who have been called by the Lord our God."*
>
> *Then Peter continued preaching for a long time, strongly urging all his listeners, "Save yourselves from this crooked generation!"*
>
> *Those who believed what Peter said were baptized and added to the church that day—about 3,000 in all. (Acts 2:37-41)*

Did you notice what happened? On the first day on the job, Peter spoke in the power of the Holy Spirit, people noticed that he had something special, and asked how they could have the same thing. Consequently, three thousand people were saved.

Peter's words pierced their heart and hit them where they lived. That is what happens when we are *Unapologetic Ambassadors for Christ*.

The problem is that it is not happening very often today. Individuals, and consequently churches, are powerless. Lives are not being transformed like that day when Peter first preached. Many followers of Christ make little impact on their friends and neighbors. I think I'm correct in saying that something is missing.

Therefore, we need to ask why we are failing. What is the cause of the power vacuum in our lives, and in the life of our churches? Perhaps it is us. Brennan Manning, theologian and writer said, "The greatest single cause of atheism in the world today is Christians who acknowledge Jesus with their lips, walk out the door, and deny Him by their lifestyle. That is what an unbelieving world simply finds unbelievable."

The first problem is not knowing enough of the truth.

If you are a true believer, a genuine follower of Christ, then you know the basics of the faith. You know that Jesus is the Son of God, and He died on a cross to save us from the consequences of our sin. You probably also know that He expects us to live a certain way, but you might not know what that really means or how it is done. You know that you are expected to believe certain things are right or wrong, but you might not know the specifics. In other words, you have at least a very basic knowledge of the truth.

However, what if a seriously inquisitive friend or neighbor asks why Jesus had to die? Or perhaps a co-worker wants to know why Christians believe certain doctrines, or someone you meet at a restaurant asks if you believe people who don't accept Jesus are going to hell. Do you know how to respond to these questions?

It is not unusual for Christians to be ignorant of many of the basic doctrines of the faith. Even many who grew up in church and attended Bible study classes all their life are not good students of the Bible.

The Book of Acts records a fascinating experience with a group of people known as Bereans.

> *And the people of Berea were more open-minded than those in Thessalonica, and they listened eagerly to Paul's message. They searched the Scriptures day after day to see if Paul and Silas were teaching the truth. As a result, many Jews believed, as did many of the prominent Greek women and men. (Acts 17:11-12)*

When they heard the Gospel preached by Paul, they turned to the Scriptures to learn the truth. They did this "day after day."

Since you first heard and responded to the Gospel, have you searched the scriptures "day after day?" Are you a student of God's Word? If not, that is probably one of the primary reasons you are not an *Unapologetic Ambassador for Christ*. An ambassador cannot be effective if he is ignorant.

One of the most famous evangelists from the early twentieth century was Billy Sunday. With flowing words he pictured his approach to the Bible:

> *I entered through the portico of Genesis and walked down through the Old Testament's art gallery, where I saw the portraits of Joseph, Jacob, Daniel, Moses, Isaiah, Solomon and David hanging on the wall; I entered the music room of the Psalms and the Spirit of God struck the keyboard of my nature until it seemed to me that every reed and pipe in God's great organ of nature responded to the harp of David, and the charm of King Solomon in his moods.*

> *I walked into the business house of Proverbs.*

I walked into the observatory of the prophets and there saw photographs of various sizes, some pointing to far-off stars or events—all concentrated upon one great Star which was to rise as an atonement for sin.

Then I went into the audience room of the King of Kings, and got a vision from four points—from Matthew, Mark, Luke and John. I went into the correspondence room, and saw Peter, James, Paul and Jude, penning their epistles to the world. I went into the Acts of the Apostles and saw the Holy Spirit forming the Holy Church, and then I walked into the throne room and saw a door at the foot of a tower and, going up, I saw One standing there, fair as the morning, Jesus Christ, the Son of God, and I found this truest friend that man ever knew; when all were false I found him true.[1]

This is a beautiful image of what it means to have a hunger for the truth. In order to know scripture we must read it frequently and interpret it meticulously.

The second problem is not living according to the truth.

Understanding scripture is not the end of the task. It is not enough. In fact, to know God's word and not allow it to impact our life is the very definition of hypocrisy. You have heard people, perhaps your friends and family members, refer to Christians as "hypocrites."

---

1   William T. Ellis, Billy Sunday, the Man and His Message, Philadelphia: The John C. Winston Co., 1917, pp.259-260.

The origination of the word "hypocrite" is the Greek theater. In those days, actors wore masks that represented their character. In other words, a man could easily fill a woman's role by simply wearing a mask. The actor was identified by the word "hypocrite." It came to describe a person who pretends to be one thing, but in reality is something else. It means to live inconsistently with our identity.

Consequently, once we hear and understand God's will, it is time to act; to take a stand. Thus, the authentic question becomes, "What should we do?" By the way, this is the exact questioned posed to Peter after he preached the truth about Jesus (see Acts 2:37).

Peter responded by giving them three tasks:

Repent of Sins

We have a tendency to think of repentance as feeling sorry that we have sinned. Repentance might begin with sorrow over sin, but it is far more. The term "repent" means to change directions. To repent of our sins means to turn away from our sins. It is not enough to feel guilty for something we do; it is not repentance until we stop doing it. Repentance causes a visible difference in the way we live.

Turn to God

Once again, it is not enough if we simply stop sinning. Let me offer an example to help us understand this concept. Let's say a man feels guilty for mistreating or abusing his wife. The guilt is powerful enough that it causes him to stop, perhaps even to offer his wife an apology and beg for her forgiveness. However, it is not complete repentance until he turns to God.

A great way to understand this concept of repentance is to picture a squadron of soldiers marching on a parade ground. They are all in step, marching in the same direction. Then the drill sergeant barks out the order, "To the rear, march!"

How do the soldiers respond? They turn completely around and march in the other direction. It is a complete change of direction. They don't just stop marching north; they stop marching north and begin to march south. That is what the Bible describes as repentance. We stop living our lives toward sin and begin to live our lives toward God.

Follow Him Publicly

The third thing Peter instructed them to do was the "be baptized in the name of Jesus." The issue of baptism has certainly been one of controversy throughout the history of the church. However, for the purpose of my discussion about being an *Unapologetic Ambassador for Christ*, I simply state that Peter instructed followers of Jesus to make a public statement of their allegiance and faith in Christ.

In the first century when Peter spoke, there was no more public expression of Jesus as Lord than to be baptized in His name. Such a public declaration often resulted in persecution and even death.

If we are going to live out what we believe, we cannot do it in secret. It is imperative that the public—our family and friends especially—know about our faith. We are not to be secretive followers of Jesus. I'm not saying you have to grab a soap box and stand on a street corner preaching Jesus, but you must speak out for your faith, and live out your beliefs.

As our knowledge of God's Word grows, and our consistency in living out God's Word develops we will begin to mature. You will begin to notice that some of your childish characteristics disappear. These characteristics include:

Being the center of your own universe. Until you mature in your faith, you will never be able to interact with those who disagree with your faith. Immature people turn every disagreement into a battle.

Insensitivity to the needs of others. Immature people are focused solely on their own needs and oblivious to those around them.

Demanding your own way. The natural reaction to the previous two items.

- Throwing temper tantrums.
- Unreasonable.
- Irresponsible.
- Responding only to concrete authority. Like a child who only obeys when threatened with punishment.

As we grow as Christians we realize it is not all about us. God loved the world (John 3:16), not just me. Before we become Christians we are too ready to condemn the world, to forget about the world. But that changes with spiritual maturity and we begin to love the world as God loves the world.

John McArthur said, "It is self defeating to proclaim the message of salvation from sin, while living a sinful lifestyle." The messenger must manifest the power of the message he is proclaiming. The dictionary defines lifestyle as being made up of your habits, attitudes, tastes, moral standards, and your economic level that together constitute the mode of living of an individual or group.

Jesus perfectly lived the truth He taught. When we fail to do the same, we destroy our effectiveness as an ambassador.

Jesus said to the crowds and to his disciples, "The teachers of religious law and the Pharisees are the official interpreters of the law of Moses. So practice and obey whatever they tell you, but don't follow their example. For they don't practice what they teach. (Matthew 23:1-3)

Reflections:

What would it take for you to become confident in your knowledge of the Word of God?

Are there any actions/activities in your life that would cause others to accuse you of being a hypocrite?

Would you use the word "mature" to describe your faith? If not, what do you need to do?

Section 2

The Christian's Relationship to the World

In the early church the message of the gospel was not spread by missionaries. It was spread primarily by traders, personal service professionals, slaves, domestic workers, cooks, butlers—people we would call marketplace people. So it immediately had a social impact!

Historian Edward Gibbon in his classic work, "The Decline and Fall of the Roman Empire" cites five reasons for Christianity's influence on the Roman Empire. In this section, we will study these reasons, and how they apply to our modern day faith.

Convictions: A Solid Foundation

You are the salt of the earth. But what good is salt if it has lost its flavor? Can you make it salty again? It will be thrown out and trampled underfoot as worthless. You are the light of the world—like a city on a hilltop that cannot be hidden. No one lights a lamp and then puts it under a basket. Instead, a lamp is placed on a stand, where it gives light to everyone in the house. In the same way, let your good deeds shine out for all to see, so that everyone will praise your heavenly Father. (Matthew 5:13-16)

In 1972, the Supreme Court issued a fascinating ruling on a case involving Christian education. An Amish man by the name of Yoder, who lived in Wisconsin, wanted to educate his children according to his religious beliefs and customs. He informed the state of Wisconsin that he would not be sending his children to school any longer.

In reply, the state claimed he could not do that because it was a violation of truancy laws. In spite of threats to sue and put him in jail, Mr. Yoder remained adamant, and refused to send his children to school. Ultimately the state took it to court and won the decision.

However, Yoder still refused after the court's ruling and filed an appeal. He also lost the appeal, but it still did not change his position. Ultimately the case landed at the bench of the Supreme Court. Finally, Mr. Yoder was heard, and the court ruled in his favor.

The Court's ruling was based on the First Amendment rights granted to Mr. Yoder. In their ruling, the court made a distinction between a "Conviction" and a "Preference." This is important for us to understand because it serves as a useful way to understand something about our beliefs and the way we behave.

A preference is a very strong belief. It might be so strong that it can control decisions you make about your life, for example, choosing to be a minister of the Gospel, or a missionary, or a teacher. It might even be such a strong belief that you are willing to spend all your money and resources according to that preference. For some, this preference can be so strong that it will cause you to want others to understand and be guided by this preference. It goes without mentioning that it will guide how you teach your children.

However, what makes it a preference rather than a conviction is that it is susceptible to change given the right circumstances. For example, it is quite common for a person to change a preference due to peer pressure. Once they discover this preference made their friends uncomfortable, they are likely to change the preference.

Let me offer an example. Let's say you have a strong belief that Christians should proclaim the Gospel boldly, wherever they go. However, you find that when you stand on the street corner collaring passersby, or you buttonhole people at the office party, your friends are embarrassed and stay away from you. At this point, many people will change their beliefs about sharing their faith. A preference is susceptible to this type of change.

Another circumstance that causes us to change a preference is family pressure. A spouse or a parent can be very influential in shaping your beliefs; even causing you to unsettle what you thought was a settled belief. There are other strong pressures we face that can cause us to change our belief about something. The court ruling identified one of the defining marks of a preference is the ability to change

On the other hand, the court ruling declared that a "conviction" is a belief that you will not change. The court suggested that a conviction will not be altered because the individual believes that it is ordained and ordered by God. A "conviction is when a belief is beyond change because it is something God has established."

Let's return to our example of proclaiming the Gospel. If your belief in the need to proclaim the Gospel is the result of believing God has ordered you to do so, you will not be deterred by pressure from friends, family, or anyone else. Later in the book (see chapter titled "Respect) we will discuss the three Israelite slaves who were thrown into the fiery furnace for refusing to bow to the king. However, remember that even in the face of the enormous pressure of a painful death they refused to give up their belief. This belief was not simply a "preference," it was a "conviction."

A conviction will motivate and guide us in spite of all opposition. We will not be deterred in a belief if it is truly a conviction. A conviction is something you purpose in your heart as the fabric of your belief system. To violate it will be considered sin.

The test of a conviction is that it will always appear in a person's lifestyle. What is truly on the inside will show on the outside. Preferences can be covered up when they are inconvenient, but a conviction will always show itself.

> *Now someone may argue, "Some people have faith; others have good deeds." But I say, "How can you show me your faith if you don't have good deeds? I will show you my faith by my good deeds." You say you have faith, for you believe that there is one God. Good for you! Even the demons believe this, and they tremble in terror. How foolish! Can't you see that faith without good deeds is useless? (James 2:17-18)*

Our true convictions will become evident with the way we live.

Here is a simple illustration of the differences between a Preference and a Conviction:

A Preference is...
- Changeable
- Negotiable
- Weakens under pressure

A Conviction is...
- Unchangeable
- Non-negotiable
- Strengthens under pressure

It is imperative that we understand this distinction because we are striving to be *Unapologetic Ambassadors for Christ*. A person who lives according to Preferences rather than Convictions will be apologetic about his faith. In fact, his faith might change if given the right circumstances.

Jesus used two images to describe His followers—salt and light. In Matthew 5, He identifies us the "salt of the earth." This is a powerful analogy when you think about salt. This mineral has three functions.

First, it is used for purifying. It is interesting that water softeners use salt to remove certain minerals from the water to make it more drinkable. Salt makes the water better, more pure. Our role as the salt of the earth is to make it better, more pure. Christians are to make the world a better place.

Historically, this has been true. Many of the great advances throughout history have been championed by followers of Christ. The world is filled with hospitals, orphanages, and rescue centers because of Christians. *Unapologetic Ambassadors for Christ* have made a remarkable difference in the world.

A second function of salt is preservation. In the time before refrigeration, meat was preserved by packing it in salt. The meat is covered with salt allowing it to draw out the moisture and preventing bacteria. If it is done correctly, meat can last for years without spoiling.

As the "salt of the earth," one of the functions of Christians is to serve as a preservative, standing against evil individuals and movements that would destroy the world. This is not to suggest we do it with swords and spears, but more likely with our witness and word.

A third function of salt is seasoning. This is so obvious that it needs little explanation. Most restaurants and cafes have salt available on the table. Nearly every recipe calls for the addition of salt to enhance taste. This would be a tasteless world without salt. Salt doesn't compromise because it knows its purpose and identity. Salt never takes on the character of that which it is seasoning.

Jesus is telling us that where there is strife, we are to be peacemakers; where there is sorrow, we are to be the ministers binding up wounds and easing pain, and where there is hatred, we are to exemplify the love of Christ, returning good for evil. This is the work of an *Unapologetic Ambassador for Christ*.

However, it is possible for the salt to "lose its flavor" and become tasteless. Picture Jesus standing near the Dead Sea as he made this statement. The Dead Sea was filled with useless salt. This salt has no purpose or value and provides a warning to us that if we fail to hold to our convictions we will become just as powerless and useless.

The second image used by Jesus is to call His followers the "light of the world." He speaks specifically of a city on a hill. If you have lived your life in the city this illustration might not resonate with you, but if you travel to the interior of this country, perhaps in western Kansas or west Texas, where you can see for miles, a town can be seen from a distance of many miles and the light will attract the traveler.

Jesus also speaks about the foolishness of covering a candle with a bushel basket. If we have light it makes no sense to keep it hidden. This is a tragic analogy of a disciple keeping his faith a secret, hidden from family and friends.

You are the salt that flavors and enhances the life of your family and friends. You are the light that guides them to the truth that can revolutionize their life. When we spread our salt and shine our light, we are doing the work of an *Unapologetic Ambassador for Christ*. This can only be done when we live according to our convictions about Jesus and His word.

When God lights you, He plans on showing you off. He wants the world to see what He is capable of doing (chain breaker, wound healer, hear mender, bondage remover, healer, redeemer, etc.).

A popular misconception about Rosa Parks is that she was an elderly woman who was just too tired to give up her seat on the bus. The truth is that she was a 42 year old secretary for the local chapter of the NAACP. She had recently attended a training session for civil rights workers. Her refusal to give up her seat was a calculated stance based on her convictions. In her autobiography, Parks said, "People always say that I didn't give up my seat because I was tired, but that isn't true. I was not tired physically, or no more tired than I usually was at the end of a working day. I was not old, although some people have an image of me as being old then. I was forty-two. No, the only tired I was, was tired of giving in."

Speaking about her conviction, Parks said, "When that white driver stepped back toward us, when he waved his hand and ordered us up and out of our seats, I felt a determination to cover my body like a quilt on a winter night."

Her actions that day changed the civil rights movement in the country, and shaped future generations. That is the power of a conviction.

Thomas Carlyle said, "Conviction is worthless unless it is converted into conduct." This is not always easy because it will often mean that our lifestyle is different from those around us. An ambassador of the United States, even if assigned to a third-world country filled with poverty, does not live like the people in that country. He lives according to the one he represents. For us, even though we are in this world, we are not to live according to this world. We are in this world, but we represent one from another world.

Reflections:

Describing your own faith, which word is more accurate: Preference or Conviction?

Can you identify anything that would cause you to give up your faith in Christ?

Describe a time in your life when you stood up for your belief even though you were alone and in opposition to the opinion of others?

Improvement: A Changed Life

Early Christian writers made some fascinating observations about the early church that should grab our attention today. Tertullian, who was known as the "Father of Latin Christianity," and wrote extensively about Christianity, spoke about the attitude and atmosphere within the church in the first three centuries. The Roman culture took note, and Tertullian wrote that the Romans would exclaim, "See how they love one another!"

Justin Martyr, who wrote even earlier than Tertullian, said, "We who used to value the acquisition of wealth and possessions more than anything else now bring what we have into a common fund and share it with anyone who needs it. We used to hate and destroy one another and refused to associate with people of another race or country. Now, because of Christ, we live together with such people and pray for our enemies."

Clement, a man who died at the very end of the first century described Christians with these words: "He impoverishes himself out of love, so that he is certain he may never overlook a brother in need, especially if he knows he can bear poverty better than his brother. He likewise considers the pain of another as his own pain. And if he suffers any hardship because of having given out of his own poverty, he does not complain."

Another early Christian, Cyprian, met an actor who had become a follower of Christ. Because the theater of the day was filled with immorality and pagan idolatry, he was encouraged to give up his association with the theater, thus his source of provisions. However, Cyprian, who was the acting Bishop of the area, instructed the church that they should be willing to support the actor if he had no other means of earning a living. He wrote, "If your church is financially unable to support him, he may move over to us and here receive whatever he needs for food and clothing."

In the midst of devastating plagues, destructive natural disasters, and wartime atrocities, Christians have often been the first to step in and risk their lives in order to help. The love of early Christians wasn't limited to fellow believers. Christians served non-believers: the poor, the orphans, the elderly, the sick, and even their persecutors.

Consequently, it is not surprising that Christianity spread quickly in those early days, in spite of persecution and other obstacles. There was something about the life of believers that attracted others. These early followers were truly *Unapologetic Ambassadors for Christ*.

The description of the very early days of the church provided in the Book of Acts helps us understand what made them so powerful. In these words, perhaps we can discover some things that can help us experience that same kind of influence in our world.

All the believers devoted themselves to the apostles' teach-ing, and to fellowship, and to sharing in meals (including the Lord's Supper), and to prayer. A deep sense of awe came over them all, and the apostles performed many miraculous signs and wonders. And all the believers met together in one place and shared everything they had. They sold their property and possessions and shared the money with those in need. They worshiped together at the Temple each day, met in homes for the Lord's Supper, and shared their meals with great joy and generosity—all the while praising God and enjoying the goodwill of all the people. And each day the Lord added to their fellowship those who were being saved. (Acts 2:42-47)

Believer's Preparation

The amazing experiences of the early church did not just happen in spite of the believers. As we see in the first words of this text, they created the environment that put them in a place to experience God's blessings. The experiences were character-ized by...

Study – Devoting themselves to the Apostles' teaching in-dicates they listened to the Twelve as they taught God's Word, which they possessed in what we call the Old Testament, and as the Apostles related their own personal experiences with Jesus. We have already discussed the value of knowing the Word of God in order to be able to do the will of God. Don't expect to be on the receiving end of many of God's blessings if you are a stranger to His Word.

Fellowship - They shared their lives together. As we see from reading further in the Book of Acts, this was far more than an occasional covered dish dinner in the church fellowship hall. They shared their lives together. The word used here is one you might be familiar with—*kononia*. It is much more than playing dominoes or charades at a party. It describes the way we share our lives with friends and close family.

Worship - This gleaned from how they shared meals together, specifically the "Lord's Supper." One of the most visible acts of worship we can experience is to share the meal together that commemorates the death of Jesus on our behalf. The early church took seriously Jesus instructions to continually observe this act as a powerful reminder of what He has done for us.

Prayer - Prayer is a reminder of how important it is to have open communication with God. Bringing us into this kind of relationship is what Jesus accomplished through His death, and if we want to create an environment where God can bless us, it is crucial that we speak with Him often. We have not talked about prayer to this point, but I will say that a vibrant, consistent prayer life is crucial if we are to be unapologetic in our walk with Christ.

These four activities (Bible study, fellowship, worship, and prayer) will create a climate of growth for individuals and for the church as a whole. The next thing we notice in Acts 2 is a description of the environment.

God's Presence

"A deep sense of awe came over them all, and the apostles performed many miraculous signs and wonders."

The word that is translated as "awe" literally means fear. It is not the kind of fear that makes us run for cover or lash out violently. Instead, it is the kind of fear that we experience when we are in the presence of something amazing and powerful. This kind of fear is a frequent occurrence when God is around.

- When Moses realized he was standing on holy ground and heard "I am the God of your father—the God of Abraham, the God of Isaac, and the God of Jacob," he covered his face because he was afraid to look at God (Exodus 3:6).

- When Jacob awoke from his dream about the ladder to heaven, he awoke from his sleep and said, "Surely the LORD is in this place, and I wasn't even aware of it!" But he was also afraid and said, "What an awesome place this is! It is none other than the house of God, the very gateway to heaven!" (Genesis 28:16-17)

- Hear the words of Isaiah when he encountered God's presence in the temple: "Then I said, 'It's all over! I am doomed, for I am a sinful man. I have filthy lips, and I live among a people with filthy lips. Yet I have seen the King, the LORD of Heaven's Armies'" (Isaiah 6:5).

- After Jesus calmed the storm, the disciples knew they were in the presence of God. They were terrified and amazed. "Who is this man?" They asked each other. "When he gives a command, even the wind and waves obey him!" (Luke 8:25).

When the early church was faithful with Bible study, fellowship, worship, and prayer they experienced the awe that comes from the presence of God in their midst. As we will note later in this passage, it was such an amazing thing that those outside the church noticed something special was happening. How could they not notice because the believers performed many "miraculous signs and wonders."

Believer's Response

As you might imagine, the early Christians wanted to remain in this condition so they were drawn together. In fact, perhaps the one word that best describes their response to God's presence is the word "together." They shared their provisions and they shared their lives. They worshipped together, they visited in each other's homes, and they shared their possessions to meet the needs of one another.

> And all the believers met together in one place and shared everything they had. They sold their property and possessions and shared the money with those in need. They worshiped together at the Temple each day, met in homes for the Lord's Supper, and shared their meals with great joy and generosity—all the while praising God and enjoying the goodwill of all the people.

There have been some over the years who have taken this passage to advocate some type of socialism practiced by the early church. I don't want to get drawn into an extended debate on this issue, but let me simply say, these early believers voluntarily shared their possessions when there was a need. This practice was not found in other Christian communities in the history of the early church. It seems clear that it was a unique response to the special circumstances surrounding a large influx of new believers in Jerusalem.

What the surrounding community recognized was the tremendous care that Christians had for one another. It was a beautiful picture of generosity and love. This is still the appropriate response to the presence of God in our midst—to give generously and love one another.

Amazing Outcome

The result of all of this was that God added new believers every day. People were constantly being saved. That is what we are striving to realize as the church today. This passage demonstrates what happens when God's people live as *Unapologetic Ambassadors for Christ*. The Word was faithfully spread and people came to saving faith in Jesus every day.

Keep this picture of the early church in mind as you read the following words of Jesus:

Your love for one another will prove to the world that you are my disciples. (John 13:35)

The early church presents a much different picture than what we see today. We expect that each family's income, bank account, house, car, property is their own personal business, completely isolated from anyone else in the church. If one family makes more money and has a bigger house and lives in a nicer neighborhood with more luxury items while another family lives on a single-mother's part-time income, food stamps, discount groceries, and a beat-up car or no car at all, then that's just their business. To each his own and do what you can for yourself and your family. Those outside your immediate family are more or less on their own.

When you describe it like this we get uncomfortable, but it is pretty accurate. At the most, each family gives to the church (maybe even a tithe or an additional offering beyond the tithe). But a very large portion of that goes to pastoral and administrative salaries, maintenance, utilities, and mortgages for the church itself. Only a small portion is set aside for the poor, and typically in the form of a benevolence account, an old clothes closet, or canned food bank.

The life of Christ offers an improved quality of life; one that moves us beyond the need to collect and accumulate for ourselves. This improved life provides the ability to give our stuff to those who have needs so they too can experience blessings.

I'm sure you remember the story of Zaccheus in the New Testament (see Luke 19:1-10). He was a Roman tax-collector who heard that Jesus was coming through his home town. He wanted to get a glimpse of this man he had heard so much about, however, he was short and unliked, so he knew he would not be allowed a front-row seat.

He climbed a tree, hoping to just see, and possibly hear a few words from Jesus. Was he surprised! Jesus stopped at the foot of the tree where Zaccheus was positioned, called him by name, and commanded him to come down. He did, and he met Jesus face to face, and his life was dramatically changed.

We know his life was changed because of what he did in response. He gave away his possessions to the poor, and made restoration with anyone he might have wronged with his tax-collecting methods.

Wow! What a change. But that is exactly what being saved is all about. It changes us. Where once we were self-consumed, trying to accumulate for ourselves, we become generous to others and lovers of all. When this happens, as it so clearly did among the early believers in Jerusalem, people notice. It is at that moment we become effective ambassadors for Christ.

Reflections:

What qualities do you exemplify that your friends and family will point to that illustrate your life in Christ is different from non-believers?

When you encounter a person in need, what is your initial response?

In what ways does your life show generosity toward others?

Humanitarianism: Caring for Others

Heal the sick, and tell them, 'The Kingdom of God is near you now.' (Luke 10:9)

Peter and John went to the temple one afternoon to take part in the three o'clock prayer service. As they approached the Temple, a man lame from birth was being carried in. Each day he was put beside the temple gate, the one called the Beautiful Gate, so he could beg from the people going into the Temple.

When he saw Peter and John about to enter, he asked them for some money. Peter and John looked at him intently, and Peter said, "Look at us!"

The lame man looked at them eagerly, expecting some money. But Peter said, "I don't have any silver or gold for you. But I'll give you what I have. In the name of Jesus Christ the Nazarene, get up and walk!"

Then Peter took the lame man by the right hand and helped him up. And as he did, the man's feet and ankles were instantly healed and strengthened. He jumped up, stood on his feet, and began to walk! Then, walking, leaping, and praising God, he went into the Temple with them.

All the people saw him walking and heard him praising God. When they realized he was the lame beggar they had seen so often at the Beautiful Gate, they were absolutely astounded! (Acts 3:1-10)

We know that he had been lame from birth, suggesting he had some type of birth defect, which kept him from ever standing on his own two feet. Perhaps for as long as two, three, or even four decades he had been carried from place to place. All of his life he was dependent upon the care of other people. He could not get up to leave a room without family and friends.

He existed in a paradoxical situation. As a male member of his family, he knew the only way to maintain his dignity was to be a breadwinner. At the same time, the only way to earn money was by begging, an occupation for those who have lost their dignity.

However, necessity won out, and every day his friends would carry him to the temple gate called "Beautiful." He would take his place among other helpless victims, hoping to catch the eye of a few temple worshippers. Do you notice the irony of placing those considered grotesque by the world in front of a place designated "Beautiful."

As he sat in a position that had become all too familiar, this lame man had already been about the task of begging for many hours. The sun had long since crossed the sky, and the morning shadows were eaten by the bright reflection from the temple walls. Several hours earlier, friends had brought a cool drink, but its effects quickly dissipated. Now, all he had to look forward to was someone coming to help him make his way home for the evening.

Placing his hand inside his pouch, the lame man fingered the few coins that had been tossed his direction by uncaring, duty-bound temple visitors. It had not been a very productive day, but truthfully, no day is worthwhile when it must be spent begging for a few tokens. He pondered his future, and slowly slipped into despair, realizing that he might spend another twenty years in this same spot.

It was nearly three o'clock with several hours of sunlight left, so the beggar put his thoughts aside, and returned to the task at hand. There was still time to turn a profit. The "ninth hour" was the "hour of prayer," and there would be an influx of people entering the gate. He needed to put forth his best efforts.

Two men approaching the temple at a brisk pace caught his eye. Their path would bring them within a few feet of his outstretched, crippled legs. As they got close enough to hear his cry, the lame man, using his most pitiful voice, captured their attention with his request for alms.

As they stopped in front of the man and looked down at his face, he knew he was about to receive a sizable donation. Seldom did he ever have a face-to-face encounter. Usually, people casually tossed coins in his direction without even a glance.

His expectations quickly turned to disappointment as he heard one of the men say, "I do not possess silver and gold..." Why did they stop? Was this some kind of cruel hoax? Did they just pause to offer sympathy? He didn't need sympathy, he needed money!

Yet, these two men, Peter and John, gave this lame man something far more valuable than gold and silver. They even awarded something worth more than health. Before we look at the prize given to the lame man, it is important to notice something about Peter and John that made their gift possible.

Everything that occurred in this encounter between Peter, John, and the lame man is built upon the foundation of prayer. Peter and John were going to the temple to pray. The healing of the lame man was made possible because of their commitment to pray. Prayer is more than a closing statement to a worship service or an opening statement at a meal.

Prayer equips us for effective ministry to the world. As we think about ministry to the world, we are prepared through prayer. We marvel at the power and effectiveness of the early church. It is important to realize that they operated on the power of prayer. Through prayer, we are equipped to make a difference in our world. We can anticipate that God will accomplish significant ministry through our lives. As we examine the healing of this lame man, we will discover the effects of prayer on our ministry.

Equips Us to Recognize the Needs of Others

When you pray for your ministry, one of the things you can expect is a new sensitivity. You will have a heightened awareness of the spiritual, physical, and emotional needs of people around you.

How many people walked into the temple that afternoon without even noticing the crippled man? Day after day, perhaps for years, this man had occupied the same spot, and no one ever really noticed his need.

Now, for some reason, Peter and John saw him from a whole new perspective. These were men of prayer, going to a place of prayer, equipped by the power of prayer. Consequently, they now saw needs around them that were concealed to everyone else.

From a spiritual perspective, we need to get to the point of recognizing the real needs of people around us. We walk by them every day and do not notice. Hurting people are all around us. They are our neighbors, co-workers, friends, and family members. We encounter them at the mall, in the office, at the ball game, everywhere we go.

Perhaps the reason we do not see their need is because our eyes have not been opened to the possibility of ministry. As you commit yourself to ministry based upon prayer, expect to have new insight into the needs of others.

Empowers Us to Respond To the Needs of Others

The disappointment of the crippled man as he heard Peter say, "I do not possess silver and gold..." was quickly changed. Peter finished his sentence with these words, "...but what I do have I give to you. In the name of Jesus Christ the Nazarene—walk!"

He did not have time to even think about the meaning of these words. Immediately he began to feel a new strength in his legs. The useless limbs began to move, and he was overwhelmed with a sense of divine power. Peter reached out and took the lame man's hand. With the strength of a man who had hauled in numerous nets filled with fish, Peter lifted the man to his feet. At that very moment, "his feet and ankles were strengthened."

Listen to the next few words and try to capture the emotion of this experience. "And with a leap, he stood upright and began to walk..." Perhaps you cannot realize the joy of being able to walk, but now, for the first time in his life, this man knew!

I mentioned earlier that Peter and John gave him something worth much more than health. They gave him freedom. For the first time in his life, he was free. The bondage to his crippled legs; the bondage to dependence on other people; the bondage to being confined to a place was suddenly gone.

By living within the confines of prayer, Peter and John were empowered to respond to the needs of this man. Through prayer we appropriate the power of God for ministry.

As you approach ministry motivated by prayer, expect to enjoy this same power and ability. Just as Peter and John, men of prayer, were able to make a difference in the lame man's life, we will have that same effectiveness. Lives will be forever changed because we minister in the power of God.

Enables Us to Rejoice In the Health of Others

Once the crippled man overcame the shock of being able to stand on his own two feet, he led a strange looking procession into the temple. His actions are described by two words:

Walking

Three times this man is described as walking. He was enjoying the freedom given to him by God. It was probably hours before he was able to sit down. Try to imagine the joy of this man, of his family and friends as he walked and jumped with his new found strength.

Praising

The second term that describes his actions is "praising." This man is leading the chorus of praises to God, but he is certainly not alone. We are told that "all the people...were filled with wonder and amazement." It was a spontaneous worship service.

Peter and John, the ones who had provided the ministry of healing, certainly became a part of this rejoicing. Do you know the joy of having a positive impact on someone's life? This kind of powerful ministry brings a feeling of satisfaction that can be found in nothing else.

When you minister under the leadership of God, and with the power of God, it will impact people's lives. Often you will never know the effect of your ministry. However, there will be times when the impact is immediate and obvious. The rejoicing that occurs will be a wonderful experience.

There is no greater thrill than to praise God alongside someone who has found wholeness in Jesus Christ. As you move out of your prayer into a ministry in the world, expect to have great times of rejoicing with neighbors and friends. Their lives will be forever changed because your ministry has been forever changed.

Gregory McPherson had a free afternoon so he took his three stepchildren to the creek to go fishing. The youngsters soon tired of the creek and began to explore the surroundings. Their father warned them not to go too far, but as is often true with children, their definition of far did not match his.

Twelve-year-old Melissa led the way for Bud, age nine and little brother Austin, only 5. They decided to climb the rocky incline that led to a train trestle, twenty feet above the creek. The curious children made it to the bridge and determined to walk the length of the track to the other side of the shore.

Still fishing in the quiet shallow creek below, Greg was unaware the children were so far away. The first thing that caught his attention was the booming sound of the train whistle as it rounded the corner. The engineer spotted the children in the middle of the bridge and sounded a futile warning.

The kids reacted quickly, grabbed hands, and began to run to the far side of the bridge. Greg, realizing what was happening, felt helpless twenty feet below the bridge. All that he could do was scream for them to run faster. His shouts were drowned out by the sound of the roaring train. He stood helplessly as the three children, running hand in hand, were overtaken by the massive train.

This is one of the most tragic stories I have ever heard. Yet it reminds me of the way we often are as Christians, standing by helplessly, as those around us are being overtaken by destruction. Our shouts to run for safety are unheeded, and we watch people struggle through life without the Lord Jesus Christ.

You have an opportunity to change all of that. Through prayer, God has prepared you to go into the world to make a difference. You can have an impact. Your voice will be heard because you will be speaking with the voice of God.

Reflections:

Make a list of people you know who have some type of physical need. Spend time the next few days praying for God to show how you can help meet their need.

What possessions do you have that you could give to someone in need? In prayer, ask God if you should share those possessions.

Morality: Pure Living in an Immoral World

A significant factor in the spread of the Christian faith in the early centuries is one of the genuine distinctive qualities of the Christian life. People were confronted with a new morality, one that was not based on the fear of punishment or even self-aggrandizement. It was morality based on a change within.

Years ago there was a man named Jerry McCally who was a Chicago drunk. He had a two-year-old daughter who died from malnutrition because of his neglect. His condition was so miserable that before the funeral, he stole her burial clothes in order to buy something to drink.

Several months later, while inside the Pacific Garden Mission in Chicago, God penetrated his heart and miraculously saved McCally. Before long, God called him to preach, and throughout the remainder of his life, he led thousands of people to Christ. When he died, there was not a church in Chicago large enough to hold all of the people who wanted to attend his funeral. This is an example of how God changes a life at salvation.

Genuine salvation makes a noticeable difference in how we live our lives. We can have assurance that we are saved because of the evidence of God's work in our lives. Jesus also tells us that true salvation results in doing the will of God. These words of Jesus are among the most decisive pronounced in the Gospels.

> *"Not everyone who says to Me, 'Lord, Lord' will enter the kingdom of heaven; but he who does the will of My Father who is in heaven. Many will say to Me on that day, 'Lord, Lord, did we not prophesy in Your name, and in Your name cast out demons, and in Your name perform many miracles?' And then I will declare to them, 'I never knew you; depart from Me, you who practice lawlessness'" (Matthew 7:21-23).*

Speaking about these words of our Lord, Martin Lloyd-Jones said, "These, surely, are in many ways the most solemn and solemnizing words ever uttered in this world, not only by any man, but even by the Son of God Himself. Indeed, were any man to utter such words we should feel compelled not only to criticize but even to condemn him. But they are the words spoken by the Son of God Himself, and therefore demand our most earnest attention. How often, I wonder, have we considered them, or heard a sermon on them? Must we not all plead guilty to the fact that, though we claim to believe the whole of Scripture, in practice we frequently deny much of it by ignoring it, simply because it does not pander to the flesh, or because it disturbs us. But if we really believe that this is the Word of God, we must consider it all; and especially must we be careful to avoid those specious arguments by which certain people endeavor to avoid the plain teaching of Scripture."[2]

These words of Jesus recorded in Matthew 7 describe the scene on the Day of Judgment. A large contingent of professed believers approached Jesus expecting to be allowed into the kingdom of heaven. Jesus reveals the nature of true, saving faith in His words to these who profess salvation.

QUALITIES OF THE EXCLUDED

If anyone other than Jesus spoke these words, we would probably not believe them. He spoke of many who will be surprised on judgment day. There will be "many" on that day who expect to enter the kingdom of heaven, yet they will be excluded. He reveals the characteristics of those who will be denied entrance into heaven.

First, they are identified by their correct doctrine (vs.21-22). The term "orthodox" simply means correct belief or teaching. We must be careful at this point because there can be no true salvation without orthodoxy. Unless we correctly believe we cannot be saved. There will be no one in heaven who does not believe properly about Jesus.

There are two phrases that reveal their orthodoxy. They approach Jesus with the confession, "Lord, Lord." The use of this expression indicates Jesus' identity. He is God. This is the Old Testament word for God. On judgment day, these people know

---

that Jesus is God, they accept His deity. This means they believe in His virgin birth, life, death, and resurrection.

Their words also reveal their position. If He is Lord, then He is master. He is in control and they are servants. They believe that Jesus is Lord. Their many religious deeds had also been done in Jesus' name (v.22). They did not claim to act on their own authority but under the authority of Jesus.

Not only did they believe right, they were also very busy. They preached, cast out demons, and performed miracles. Surely that should verify their sincerity. Not according to Jesus. There are many today who claim the same works and yet are probably not true disciples of Jesus.

How is it possible to do these kinds of works without being genuinely saved? On occasion, God empowers unbelievers to do miraculous things, or to speak for Him. History is filled with instances of God's miraculous revelation. Consider, for example, the highly unusual story of the prophet Balaam in the Old Testament. He was a prophet for hire who pronounced a blessing upon God's people (See Numbers 22-23). It would be a stretch to call him a man of God even though he was utilized by God.

There are others who perform these works under the power of Satan. For false Christs and false prophets will arise and will show great signs and wonders, so as to mislead, if possible, even the elect" (Matthew 24:24).

False faith is concerned with outward appearances. Genuine faith is concerned with a sincere heart. False faith produces hypocrisy (good works and an immoral life). Genuine faith produces holiness.

It will be a real tragedy when these people are exposed. They will be surprised "on that day." They are currently self-deceived and we should never add to their deception by encouraging their false assurance. Many trust their belief rather than Christ. After all their works, they must still ask, "What about my relationship to the Lord Jesus?"

The attitude of a truly saved man is exemplified by Paul.

Yes, everything else is worthless when compared with the infinite value of knowing Christ Jesus my Lord. For his sake I have discarded everything else, counting it all as garbage, so that I could gain Christ and become one with him. I no longer count on my own righteousness through obeying the law; rather, I become righteous through faith in Christ. For God's way of making us right with himself depends on faith. I want to know Christ and experience the mighty power that raised him from the dead. I want to suffer with him, sharing in his death... (Philippians 3:8-10).

If we strive after anything else, we are on the wrong road.

Quality of the Included

Only one quality of those included in the kingdom is given— they "do the will of My Father who is heaven." If doing the Father's will is necessary for salvation, then to have assurance that we are saved, we must know something about His will. John 3:16 says if we believe and confess we will have eternal life; it doesn't say anything about acts? The acts do not secure our salvation, they secure our position in heaven.

In Romans 12:1-2 we are told the conditions necessary to know God's will.

> *I urge you therefore, brethren, by the mercies of God, to present your bodies a living and holy sacrifice, acceptable to God, which is your spiritual service of worship. And do not be conformed to this world, but be transformed by the renewing of your mind, that you may prove what the will of God is, that which is good and acceptable and perfect (Romans 12:1-2).*

This text lists two things we must do which will enable us to "prove what the will of God is..."

It speaks first of a presentation (v.1). These words are understood in light of the sacrificial system of the Old Testament. A burnt offering was a voluntary gift to God, symbolic of total commitment. In order to know the will of God, we must offer a sacrifice that is living as opposed to the slain animal on the altar. Our lives are to be presented to God.

Our sacrifice must also be "holy." The term means separated or set apart for God's purposes. Our sacrifice must be "acceptable to God." This means that it meets God's requirements.

The second requirement for knowing the will of God is transformation (v.2). Prior to knowing God's will we must no longer be conformed to the world. This means that we are not attracted nor distracted by the things of the world. Rather, we are to be transformed "by the renewing of your mind." This is an experience that takes place at salvation. Our minds, our way of thinking are renewed.

He saved us, not on the basis of deeds which we have done
in righteousness, but according to His mercy, by the washing
of regeneration and renewing by the Holy Spirit (Titus 3:5).

When we have presented ourselves to God and been transformed by God, we are then able to know the will of God.

God also helps us in knowing His will by providing some
specific revelations. Scripture contains some definite things that
have been revealed as the will of God. These are things that we
know are God's will in every circumstance.

God's Word tells us that God desires that we be controlled
by the Holy Spirit.

So then do not be foolish, but understand what the will of
the Lord is. And do not get drunk with wine, for that is dissi-
pation, but be filled with the Holy Spirit (Ephesians 5:18-19).

The word "filled" simply means controlled. It means God's
will is that we allow the Holy Spirit to control our lives. Some,
who claim to be saved, are drunk with wine more than they are
filled with the Spirit of God.

Sanctification is another aspect of God's revealed will.

For this is the will of God, your sanctification; that is that you
abstain from sexual immorality (1 Thessalonians 4:3).

The term "sanctification" means to be holy, pure, or set
apart. God's will is that we live a holy life. Genuine faith results
in holiness. If our life is not characterized by holiness, then we
are not doing God's will and our faith is false.

A saved life is a changed life! To be saved you must possess
the correct doctrine of Christ. Every cult can be distinguished by

their false doctrine of Jesus. No one will be in heaven who does not believe correctly. The one with genuine faith will also be very busy serving God and His church. They will be characterized by much religious activity. However, the distinguishing mark is obedience to the will of God.

From our perspective, the distinction between those excluded from God's kingdom and those included in God's kingdom may be hard to determine. However, we can be assured that God can discern. He judges, not on the basis of religious works, but upon the basis of obedience to God's will.

Jesus is not asking us to do these things in order to be saved. He is asking if these things (doing God's will) are the desire of your heart. A saved person does God's will. Not 100% of the time, but it is the basic goal of his life.

This is why the early believers were characterized by their distinctive morality. They had been changed from the inside, which was reflected on the outside. This is what allows us to be *Unapologetic Ambassadors for Christ.*

Who is Jesus speaking to in today's world? Many who will say, "Lord, Lord, I'm a church member. I walked the isle at age 12 in church, I was baptized, attended Sunday School as a child, gave a big check to the building fund, my wife and kids go to church all the time..." All of these things can be said by one who does not possess a genuine salvation. However, genuine faith results in a lifestyle consistent with that faith.

Reflections:

What characteristics or actions that are a part of your life give you confidence of salvation?

List the ways your life has been changed since you first met Jesus?

What evidences of your relationship with Jesus can others recognize in your life?

Unity: Working Together to Serve Others

But as the believers rapidly multiplied, there were rumblings of discontent. The Greek-speaking believers complained about the Hebrew-speaking believers, saying that their widows were being discriminated against in the daily distribution of food.

So the Twelve called a meeting of all the believers. They said, "We apostles should spend our time teaching the word of God, not running a food program. And so, brothers, select seven men who are well respected and are full of the Spirit and wisdom. We will give them this responsibility. Then we apostles can spend our time in prayer and teaching the word."

Everyone liked this idea, and they chose the following: Stephen (a man full of faith and the Holy Spirit), Philip, Procorus, Nicanor, Timon, Parmenas, and Nicolas of Antioch (an earlier convert to the Jewish faith). These seven were presented to the apostles, who prayed for them as they laid their hands on them.

So God's message continued to spread. The number of believers greatly increased in Jerusalem, and many of the Jewish priests were converted, too. (Acts 6:1-7)

A significant quality of the early church that led to rapid growth in the Roman world was their unity. The union and discipline of the Christian community gradually formed an increasing influence on the heart of the Roman Empire. However, this unity was not easily attained. From the very beginning, early church leaders were challenged to find ways to overcome issues that had the potential of causing division.

Perhaps the earliest example of this possibility is seen in what has become a centuries old debate within the church about whether the primary emphasis should be on evangelism or ministry. Denominations have been formed because of this issue. Churches have split, individual believers have parted ways over which is most important.

Those who take the side of evangelism believe that the church should do little more than preach the Gospel, and once people are saved, God will provide all their material needs. Man's most pressing need is spiritual, and it is an unnecessary waste of time and resources to be concerned with the material world.

On the other side of the issue are those who place the emphasis on ministry. These folks advocate that the best way to reach the world is through social involvement and action. The church is to make the world a better place. Once we have met a person's physical needs, then we have an audience to speak to their spiritual problems.

John Stott has summarized the problem. "Too many of us evangelicals either have been, or maybe still are, irresponsible escapists. Fellowship with each other in the church is more congenial than service in an apathetic and even hostile environment outside. Of course we make occasional evangelistic raids into enemy territory (that is our evangelical specialty); but then we withdraw again, across the moat, into our Christian castle (the security of our own evangelical fellowship), pull up the drawbridge, and even close our ears to the pleas of those who batter on the gate. As for social activity, we have tended to say that is largely a waste of time in view of the imminent return of the Lord. After all, when the house is on fire, what is the point of hanging new curtains or rearranging the furniture? The only thing that we really should engage in is to rescue the perishing. Thus we have tried to salve our conscience with a bogus theology."[3]

Ministry, both its practice and neglect, can have a tremendous impact on people's lives. Charles Colson tells of meeting a prison inmate in Cardiff Wales. He was Jewish by birth, but had converted to Christianity while in college. Later he dropped out of college and found himself in the wrong crowd, getting into drugs and finally prison. Upon serving his term, with a desire to go straight, he went for help to the minister of his church. All he received was a lecture on how terrible his life had been.

"Finally," he said, "I realized that the church didn't want me—didn't trust me around young people. So I left and tried

---

3   Stott, John R. *Issues Facing Christians Today*, Zondervan, 2006, p. 24.

another church. They didn't want me either. I went back to my old friends. And here I am again, the second time in prison."[4]

The early church dealt with this same issue. The way they resolved the problem provides an effective example for us to follow. If we do, just like it allowed the first century church to be powerful witnesses for Christ, it will allow the church today to be an *Unapologetic Ambassador for Christ*.

Discovering a Specific Need vs.1-2

Up until this point, things had gone relatively smooth for the new church; however things changed when a group of people within the church began to feel neglected. Satan's most effective weapons against the church are not external, but come from within. The early church was faced with internal dissention and their response was crucial. The dispute uncovered a specific need.

Two groups of people were involved in the situation: Hellenists or "Grecians" who were non-native born Jews scattered all over the Mediterranean world. They mingled with Gentiles, spoke the Greek language, and neglected the Hebrew tongue. They were attracted to Greek theatre and Roman games. They were often drawn back to Jerusalem for religious reasons, but not readily accepted. Apparently, as a result from the phenomenon of Pentecost, some were saved and became a part of the church.

On the other hand there were Hebrew Jews, in both culture and religion. They had maintained the strict Jewish religion,

---

4 http://www.breakpoint.org/search-library/
search?view=searchdetail&id=1571

remained in the homeland, and had rejected the influence of Greek culture.

In these early days of the church, apparently there was a daily distribution of food to the widows of the community of faith. The church took seriously its obligation to care for one another. However, the Hellenistic widows were being neglected. They were not receiving equal portions with the Jewish widows. Note there was no dispute over whether the problem existed, obviously they were being overlooked. The problem was prejudice and segregation.

One of the outcomes if this problem was left unsolved would be that the apostles would have to "neglect the word of God in order to wait on tables." Those who were entrusted with the Word might have to ignore their calling to tend to this need.

In the late 19th century, evangelicals led the way in massive social reforms—cleaning up abuses in coal mines, pioneering child labor laws, introducing public education and public hospitals, and abolishing the slave trade. This is the heritage of those who are deeply concerned for evangelism.

The success of evangelism depends upon the ability to recognize those in need. Those suffering are much more responsive to the Gospel than those at ease. Uncovering a physical need is to discover an opportunity to spread the Gospel.

Defining a Specific Solution vs.3-4

The apostles responded to the need with a specific solution. They recommended the selection of seven men to concentrate on solving this problem. The responsibility for this ministry would be turned over to them. These men were not just anybody who would volunteer; they were to be men of..."good reputation." Their character was to be known by others within the church. This is a necessary quality for church leadership in order to preserve unity within the church (see 2 Cor. 8:17-18). They were also to be Spirit-filled. To be "Spirit-filled" is to be controlled by the Holy Spirit. Being Spirit-filled is the dominant theme of Acts (see Acts 2:4; 4:8,31; 7:55; 11:24; 13:9,52). Wisdom is also a prerequisite for effective ministry. Responding to the world's needs requires wisdom. If our ministry is not led by men and women gifted with wisdom it will be weak and unsuccessful.

The Twelve would now be free to be about the task they were called to—prayer and proclamation. They did not neglect ministry in favor of evangelism, but rather they found a means to effectively do both. Elton Trueblood said, "If you are a Christian, then you are a minister. A non-ministering Christian is a contradiction in terms."

This incident recorded in Scripture reveals a great truth: Both ministry and evangelism are necessary. The disciples neglected neither evangelism nor ministry; they did not emphasize one over the other. Instead, they found a solution to enable them to do both. Here is our pattern for the twenty-first century church. God equips the church to do both ministry and evangelism.

God had already provided the resources for the church to effectively minister and preach. We do not have to sacrifice one to do the other; He has provided the necessary resources.

Dedicating a Specific Ministry vs.5-6

The need was revealed and the response discovered, now the church dedicated a specific ministry to solve the problem.

This ministry was single-minded and "found approval with the whole congregation." I have often wondered if the church should operate business matters in this fashion—no decisions made until there is unanimity. It would impress upon each of us the responsibility we have to discover God's will for our church.

This list of the names of these seven men is not insignificant. They are all Greek names, indicating they were all Hellenistic Jews, with the exception of Nicolas, a Gentile convert to Judaism. It points to the willing sacrifice made by the majority Hebrews. They allowed the Hellenistic Jews to take charge of the whole distribution process, thus insuring their widows would not be neglected. They gave up all their rights in order to insure harmony within the church. The lesson here is too obvious to need mentioning.

The apostles saw this as a spiritual ministry, not just a mundane physical chore. It was approached with the same seriousness as preaching or missionary work. They prayed for these men, and laid hands upon them as a symbol of being set apart to a special office within the church.

Charles Chaney was driving through South Chicago along a side street when he saw a black man and two children on the sidewalk. It was a January morning with the temperature well below zero, and the wind was blowing hard. It was at a time when racial tensions were at a peak in the city.

Chaney pulled to the curb, opened the door, and said, "How may I help you?"

The surprised man replied that he was waiting for a bus. Chaney offered them a ride. After several minutes in the car the man finally blurted, "Why are you, a white man, offering me a ride?"

Chaney's answer was immediate, "Because Jesus Christ changed my life."

Ministry was a part of who he was in Christ. God has equipped the church to respond to every need that men and women have. We must not side-step our responsibility to serve them. Effective ministry is an open door to proclaim the Gospel to those in need.

There were an estimated 36,000 homeless in New York with only 3,500 available beds in shelters when Ed Koch was Mayor of the city. Mr. Koch appealed to the city's 3,500 churches to each take ten people to resolve the situation.

The response of the churches was unanimous—they were all shocked the Mayor would make such a request without consulting with them first. They cited the cost of heating buildings, and the inconvenience for existing church programs, and on church people as they refused to help.

The opportunities for ministry are all around us and each of them can open doors for the Gospel. God's plan for reaching the lost requires that the church be involved in effective ministry to those within and without the congregation. And when those ministries create the possibility of conflict within the church, it is imperative that we find a way to resolve the matter and preserve our unity.

Pastor Gordon MacDonald tells of driving to church early one Sunday morning. He encountered a skunk in the road that had discovered a cocoa box that probably had a few grains of chocolate in the bottom. Greed got the best of him, and his head had become stuck. Now the animal staggered around the street trying to free himself.

As MacDonald watched the scene the thought occurred to him to help the skunk, but he quickly came to his senses. He drove on, feeling the guilt of the priest and Levite traveling down the Jericho road. Later, he pondered about what might have happened to that skunk. Perhaps police came and shot him, or a braver person attempted a rescue, or perhaps he was still wandering in the woods in a dangerous situation.

MacDonald then raised the question as to why we can feel such sympathy for an animal, yet so often ignore humans in a similar predicament.

A destitute woman who was turned away by a church with the words, "We will pray for you" wrote the following poem:

I was hungry,
and you formed a humanities group to discuss my hunger.
I was imprisoned,
and you crept off quietly to your chapel and prayed for my release.
I was naked,
and in your mind you debated the morality of my appearance.
I was sick,
and you knelt and thanked God for your health.
I was homeless,
and you preached to me of the spiritual shelter of the love of God.
I was lonely,
and you left me alone to pray for me.
You seem so holy, so close to God
But I am still very hungry - and lonely - and cold.

The world is watching. They are watching to discover how we respond to those in need, and they are also observant of how we settle our differences when ministry becomes messy. In John 17, we hear Jesus' prayer for his followers, the church. It is very insightful on the necessity and power of unity.

> *I pray that they will all be one, just as you and I are one—as you are in me, Father, and I am in you. And may they be in us so that the world will believe you sent me. (John 17:21)*

If the world is to believe our message, they must first see our unity. If you are at odds with your brother or sister in Christ, or if you are angry with your church, you are not an *Unapologetic Ambassador for Christ.*

Reflections:

List some specific needs in your community that are being ignored by your church?

What are some ways that you can become involved in fulfilling those needs?

Section 3

The Opinion about Christians by the World

Attractiveness

The simplest definition of advertising is that it is an attempt to get people to buy stuff. Obviously, advertising is much more complicated than that, but once you strip away all the complexities, that is the purpose. How that goal is accomplished can become extremely complex, especially today with the proliferation of numerous types of media and communication.

The days are gone when you could purchase a few newspaper or magazine pages, or even create a radio spot. We have even moved beyond the use of television and the ultra expensive 30-second commercial. Today's advertisers create videos to promote products with the hope they will go viral, or produce hashtags that will spread the word about the product.

However, there is one form of advertising that has proven itself, and continues to be the most effective method since the beginning of advertising. I am referring to satisfied customers seen using the product. When people see others with the product and they speak of their approval, it provides advertisement that exceeds anything that can be created or purchased.

One of the most successful products in using this style of advertising is Apple. The company has certainly spent a great deal of money on traditional advertising over the years, but one of the greatest things they have going is the evangelistic style zeal of Apple users. Starting with the early Apple Computers to the current iPhones, many of us have purchased their products because our friends use them and brag about them constantly.

This kind of "word of mouth" or watching the success of the product works in many arenas. When we see others with something we would like to possess, we strive to obtain it for ourselves.

Imagine this also being true for the church. What if your family, friends, and neighbors observed you living the kind of life that is winsome because of your faith in Christ, how would they respond? No doubt, they would ask about what makes your life different, and how can they have that for themselves. Your walk with God should look so good people will want what you have.

When Simon saw that the Spirit was given when the apostles laid their hands on people, he offered them money to buy this power. "Let me have this power, too," he exclaimed, "so that when I lay my hands on people, they will receive the Holy Spirit!"

But Peter replied, "May your money be destroyed with you for thinking God's gift can be bought! You can have no part in this, for your heart is not right with God. Repent of your wickedness and pray to the Lord. Perhaps he will forgive your evil thoughts, for I can see that you are full of bitter jealousy and are held captive by sin." (Acts 8:18-23)

The context for these verses is the scattering of the early church shortly after the amazing experiences of Pentecost in Jerusalem. Persecution came under the leadership of a man named Saul, later known as Paul, and Christians were forced to flee. The story follows Phillip who preached the Gospel in Samaria. The writer tells us that "crowds listened intently to Philip because they were eager to hear his message and see the miraculous signs he did" (Acts 8:6).

The crowds were not only attracted to his message, but also by his actions. He performed amazing signs. He was especially noted for casting out evil spirits and bringing healing and health to hopeless people. It was noted so much that we are told it brought great joy to the city.

Have you ever heard of Christians doing the kind of things that would bring great joy to an entire city? When we speak of Samaria we are not talking about a place like New York City or some other modern-day metropolis. It was more like what we would think of as a small rural village. But Phillip still became the talk of the town because of his message and his method. He preached Jesus, and he ministered in the name of Jesus. He was a true definition of an ambassador for Christ.

However, Phillip was not the first person to show up in Samaria claiming to be from God. There was already a man there named Simon (not to be confused with Simon Peter). Simon already had a big following, self-identified as "Simon the Great one with the power of God." People listened to his message because he was also an adept magician.

Phillip had something so special that Simon wanted it for himself. It is probably safe to say that his motives were not pure. He was not as much interested in using the power of God's Spirit to help others as he was to line his own pockets. Imagine how much a magician could make if he had the real power of God instead of the trickery of magic.

But here's the point I want to make. This man saw something in the lifestyle and power of Phillip that he wanted for himself. This should be true of all of God's people. Our family, friends, and neighbors need to see something about our life in Christ that they would like to have for themselves.

Specifically, there are two aspects of our life that can be appealing to others. As we will discover, both are a direct consequence of the Holy Spirit at work within us.

Our Attitude

It is possible to keep our attitudes hidden. Most of us have become pretty good at covering up our depression, or pushing our anger in a closet so others are unaware. However, eventually the negative will be revealed. It might be during an experience of grief, or at a time when we are wronged. Those who know us will see through our facades and recognize our true attitudes.

The person who is controlled by God's Spirit possesses qualities that are appealing and will cause others to desire what we have.

But the Holy Spirit produces this kind of fruit in our lives: love, joy, peace, patience, kindness, goodness, faithfulness, gentleness, and self-control. There is no law against these things! (Galatians 5:22-23)

When the Holy Spirit controls our life it will be characterized by these qualities:

Love - The term used is *agape*, which refers to self-giving, self-sacrificing love. It is the kind of love God has for us that motivated Him to send His son Jesus. It is the kind of love described in the great thirteenth chapter of first Corinthians. Love is perhaps the most essential quality for a person to possess in order to be appealing to others. People are drawn to people who are loving. They will tolerate many other failings when they know we love them.

Joy - To have joy means to live in a settled state of contentment, confidence, and hope. It might refer to a feeling of pleasure, but most likely it means a sense of well-being. A person with joy exudes a quiet sense that all is well. It is not necessarily laughing out loud and telling jokes. It is the ability to live at peace, even in the midst of hostile or unpleasant circumstances. This kind of joy is from deep within, and doesn't fluctuate according to outward situations.

Peace - When we typically think of peace it conjures up images of lack of warfare or conflict. We speak of world peace to refer to not needing armies. However, the biblical concept of peace is much deeper, and speaks of an inner wholeness, to be complete, to live well. It speaks of living in a right relationship with God and with others, which brings calmness to our lives. A person who is at peace does not worry about the future or about present things. Their presence brings with it a spirit of calm that can infect others.

Patience – Biblical patience does not suggest we simply turn our back toward sin and injustice, hoping things will get better. Neither is it a stoic philosophy that essentially says, "grin and bear it." Rather than being passive toward the world and circumstances, patience is very active in that it allows us to hold on to the promises of God. We can be patient because we have God's Word and the hope it describes for the future. We don't simply ignore things; we look beyond them and see God.

Kindness – Kindness is essentially goodness in action. It is characterized by things like grace, tenderness, mercy, compassion, and self-sacrificing tender action on behalf of others. Occasionally we will have an opportunity to do a great act of kindness of someone, but every day we have the ability to perform a minor act of kindness that may or may not be noticed.

Goodness – This term is closely related to the idea of kindness, but perhaps the most notable difference is that it seems to be kindness that is more aggressive. In other words, rather than responding in kindness as we come into contact with others, it describes going out of our way to act in kindness toward others. It is making the effort to do good things.

Faithfulness – faithfulness hinges upon what we value as important and our commitment to that value. It is probably safe to say that we will be faithful to the things we think are truly important, which might include family, friendships, employer, school, sports team, or anything else we value. It means to remain true, without wavering. Within the context of the Christian life it would describe a person who remains true to God and His Word.

Gentleness – The basic meaning of this word is meekness, or humility. The tendency is to see this characteristic as a weakness, but the biblical understanding reveals it is a powerful strength. Moses is described as being "meek" (see Numbers 12:3), but there was nothing weak about a man who could stand before Pharaoh, the most powerful man in the world at the time, and demand freedom for his people. The best way to understand this term is strength under control.

Self-Control – This means to govern or control ourselves. It prevents us from striking out in anger, falling apart in sadness, or losing ourselves in silliness. It is self-mastery, to hold our appetites in check. Perhaps the opposite would be someone who is controlled by addictions.

All of these qualities are the possession of one who is filled with God's Spirit. These are the personality traits and attributes that make us appealing to others; the things that will cause them to want what we have. The person who exemplifies the fruit of the Spirit will certainly be an *Unapologetic Ambassador for Christ*.

Our Actions

People will not only be drawn to our attitude, but they will also be attracted by our actions. Just as the Holy Spirit supplies everything we need for our attitude, He also provides what we need to cause others to respond to our actions.

A spiritual gift is given to each of us so we can help each other. (1 Corinthians 12:7)

Return to the story we read at the beginning concerning Simon the magician. He was attracted to Phillip because he brought healing and wholeness through the Holy Spirit. It was the ability to physically help a person that was the attraction.

In order for all of His people to perform the type of actions that are attractive to others, God has given us spiritual gifts. The clear teaching of the New Testament is that God gives spiritual gifts to the church for the common good of the saints (1 Corinthians 12:7) and to empower her mission to evangelize (1 Corinthians 14:24–25). In other words, when we operate in the gifts of the Spirit we are doing the work of God in the world.

In 1 Corinthians 12, Paul explains that each Christian is a unique member of Christ's body, and therefore each of us has a unique function. We are capable of fulfilling our role because we receive unique gifts that benefit the "common good" of the body (see verses 7, 12, 29–30). He gives us gifts so that for the greater glory of Christ we are able to pursue love through serving one another.

When discussing spiritual gifts, the temptation is to get distracted by some of the more visible and controversial gifts. Such a discussion is not the purpose of this book other than to say that if God gives us a unique ability it is incumbent upon us to utilize that ability in ministry to others.

Much of the work of individual Christians and the church as a whole is done according to human ingenuity and talent. Consequently, it has very little impact on the world. We can use human methods and techniques to draw a crowd or put on a good show, but they are powerless to change lives. People may be attracted by our human skills, but it will only be temporary. Even Simon the magician knew how to draw a crowd. However, he recognized Jesus' disciples had something much more powerful than anything in his bag of tricks.

People notice what we do. Even those who don't know you well enough to discern the positive aspect of your attitude are able to see your actions. When we minister to others through the power of the Holy Spirit we will find ourselves doing things that will draw others to Christ. This is the reason God gives us spiritual gifts—not for our benefit, but for the purpose of fulfilling our task as ambassadors for Christ.

When all your friends are using an iPhone, and they constantly rave about what it can do and how they love everything about it, you want to go down to the phone store and get an iPhone for yourself. When you see what it does for someone else you can't help but want to experience it as well.

As believers in Christ, our walk should look so good that others are drawn to Christ. Our friends, family members, and neighbors will hear us talk about Jesus, and they will see how He has shaped our attitudes, and they will experience the blessings of our actions, and they will want what we have. That is what it means to be an *Unapologetic Ambassador for Christ.*

Reflections:

Read Galatians 5:22-23. Do you struggle with any of the qualities listed in these verses? If so, how does it affect your witness to others?

What are your spiritual gifts? In other words, what abilities do you have that God uses in a positive manner to impact others? Are you utilizing those gifts when you relate to others?

Appeal

John Harper was saved at age thirteen and began preaching at age seventeen. He had a consuming passion to share the Gospel with everyone he met. He started a church in London in 1896 (now known as Harper Memorial Church) which grew to over 500 members by the time he moved on thirteen years later.

Three times during his life, John Harper nearly met his death by drowning. At the age of two, he fell into a well and was resuscitated by his mother. At twenty-six, he was swept out to sea by a reverse current and barely survived. Six years later, he found himself on a leaking ship in the middle of the Mediterranean. Perhaps God used these events to prepare Harper for his most challenging experience.

On the night of April 14, 1912, Harper was on the R.M.S. Titanic as it sailed through the bitter cold waters of the north Atlantic. Everyone knows what happened on that fateful night as this reputedly unsinkable ship sank in the frigid water.

John Harper placed his six-year-old daughter Nina into a lifeboat, and refused invitations to take a place for himself with the girl. Looking into her eyes, he told her that she would see him again someday.

Eyewitness reports say that Harper was seen making his way up the deck yelling, "Women, children and unsaved into the lifeboats!" As the boat broke apart, Harper jumped into the water along with the remaining 1,528 passengers.

John Harper was seen swimming frantically to people in the water, leading them to Jesus before the hypothermia became fatal. He swam to one young man who had climbed on a piece of debris and between breaths asked, "Are you saved?" The young man replied that he was not.

He tried to lead him to Christ only to have the young man who was near shock reply, "No."

Harper then took off his life jacket and threw it to the man, and said, "Here then, you need this more than I do" as he swam off to talk to other people. A few minutes later he swam back to the young man and succeeded in leading him to salvation.

Four years later, at a survivors' meeting, this young man stood up, and in tears, recounted the story. He shared how that after John Harper led him to Christ; he tried to help other people. However, the cold became too intense. His last words before going under were, "Believe on the name of the Lord Jesus and you will be saved."

The fellow passengers with John Harper on the Titanic went from being people who might be interested in the Christian faith to people who desperately needed the hope of the Christian faith. This dramatic change was produced by a unique set of circumstances, but this kind of change can happen in everyday situations as well. As people watch your walk with God and how you deal with trials and tribulation, people go from wanting what you have to needing what you have.

Meanwhile, Peter traveled from place to place, and he came down to visit the believers in the town of Lydda. There he met a man named Aeneas, who had been paralyzed and bedridden for eight years.

Peter said to him, "Aeneas, Jesus Christ heals you! Get up, and roll up your sleeping mat!" And he was healed instantly.

Then the whole population of Lydda and Sharon saw Aeneas walking around, and they turned to the Lord.

There was a believer in Joppa named Tabitha (which in Greek is Dorcas). She was always doing kind things for others and helping the poor. About this time she became ill and died. Her body was washed for burial and laid in an upstairs room. But the believers had heard that Peter was nearby at Lydda, so they sent two men to beg him, "Please come as soon as possible!"

So Peter returned with them; and as soon as he arrived, they took him to the upstairs room. The room was filled with widows who were weeping and showing him the coats and other clothes Dorcas had made for them.

But Peter asked them all to leave the room; then he knelt and prayed. Turning to the body he said, "Get up, Tabitha." And she opened her eyes! When she saw Peter, she sat up! He gave her his hand and helped her up. Then he called in the widows and all the believers, and he presented her to them alive.

The news spread through the whole town, and many believed in the Lord. And Peter stayed a long time in Joppa, living with Simon, a tanner of hides. (Acts 9:32-42)

The Book of Acts records the experiences of a few disciples as they were scattered from Jerusalem by persecution. One of those characters was Peter who traveled from place to place, but eventually found himself in the town of Lydda. Something amazing happened to Peter as he ministered in that obscure village.

Appealing Ministry

Peter was the first crusade evangelist for the church, preaching that powerful sermon at Pentecost to the multitudes gathered in Jerusalem. An interesting feature of this story at Lydda is that Peter was not preaching to a large crowd, or even to a small gathering. In his private ministry he met a man named Aeneas. He is a man who had been bedridden for eight years.

This is Peter, the de facto leader of the church, yet he still had the time and opportunity to meet a man who had been crippled for nearly a decade. It would be easy to assume that Peter would have been surrounded by handlers to keep away the everyday person, but that was not the case. Peter was out among the people. He put himself in a position to meet people in need. In fact, it seems he had a ministry to these people.

Peter, with all the burdens he carried, had time for this man with a need. He was a busy man, and you know people demanded his time, and wanted to talk to him, and sit with him, and counsel with him, and have him speak for their groups. Yet God kept opening new ministries. There was never any end to it.

If you ever want to be fruitful in the ministry, you have to get in the mainstream of what God is doing. God does not go up to the shelf and dust you off for an important ministry. Start where you are. There are many things needed to be done, to pray, to teach, to minister to others needs, to use your spiritual gifts. Be about the ministry wherever you are. As you do this, you will find yourself in the middle of God's activity.

Get active in what God is doing. Go in some direction. Be involved in what the Spirit of God is doing. Don't be sitting around. Some people are idle, just twiddling their thumbs. They have no sense of commitment to active ministry. Their priorities in life are everything else. And it's God's people who are already active in what God is doing who find themselves getting new ministries all the time. Do you think God's going to dust off a spiritually lethargic person and put them in a strategic place? If you're faithful over little, he'll make you Lord over much. But you've got to start where you are.

It was no accident that Peter happened to be in the lame man's home on the day God was going to heal him. Peter was busy about ministering to people, and he was ready to be used by God.

We make a big mistake when we sit around waiting for God to call us to something big. It's like we think we are so good that God is saving us for the big stuff. God would never expect someone like me to get dirty in some inconsequential ministry. I'll be ready when God wants to use me for something amazing. But, that's not how God works. He uses people who are busy, putting themselves in places where God is doing His business.

It is in those places that we create a ministry that is appealing; the kind of ministry that causes others to realize they need what we have. Peter met a man named Aeneas who had been confined to a bed for eight years. He couldn't walk, which meant in the ancient world he was of little value to anyone. He couldn't take care of himself, and he certainly couldn't provide for anyone else.

Peter stood next to Aeneas' bed, spoke in the name of Jesus, and the man stood up and walked. First time in eight years. He was healed. Consequently, the entire population of two towns saw what happened. They knew Aeneas since he was one of them, but now they saw him get up out of his bed and walk. Word spread quickly.

Arising Need

Word about what had happen in Lydda spread to the neighboring town of Joppa where a woman named Tabitha lived (also known by her Greek name *Dorcas*). Tabitha is described as a wonderful woman, full of good works. This woman was totally devoted to good works. It seems that she made clothes for the poor and needy. She was the personification of what a Christian should be, and the word disciple is used to describe her.

This amazing woman died, and it was a very distressing time for the church. The custom of the Jews at death was immediately to bury the body, since they did not do any embalming. They would merely do what they called the washing. But in this case, they didn't bury her, which was unusual, because dead bodies were an unsacred thing in Israel to a Jew, and they didn't let dead bodies hang around. They just put her up on the second floor of the house.

The believers in Joppa heard that Peter had the ability to make a crippled man walk and realized they needed what he had. Their beloved Tabitha was dead, and if this man Peter could heal a lame man then perhaps he can raise a dead woman. So they sent word imploring Peter to come as quickly as possible. They desperately needed what he had.

This is what happens when you have a ministry that is appealing to others. It might be something others want, but under the right circumstances is goes beyond something they simply want to something they desperately need.

Amazing Response

It is important that Peter didn't excuse himself from going by saying some like this: "Well, look, I mean she died. Praise the Lord. She's with the Lord, in a much better place." But, Peter didn't do that. He got up and went, dropping everything. He was still about the business of fulfilling the ministry God had given to him.

When Peter arrived, people were gathered in her room. They couldn't wait to show all the clothes and garments Tabitha had made for others. They were grieving, but they were also celebrating the life of their departed friend. She had spent her life providing for them and they already missed her desperately.

Then Peter asked everyone to leave the room so he could be alone. I can imagine what people must have been thinking. Many were curious about what he was going to do, perhaps others felt an excitement that something special was about to happen.

All we are told is that Peter turned to the dead body and said, "Get up, Tabitha."

A simple command. She opened her eyes and Peter gave a hand as she rose to her feet. Peter then invited everyone back in the room to see their friend, freshly raised from the dead.

To be honest, it's hard to comprehend the feeling in the room at that moment. How would anyone be able to describe the emotions after such an event? The Bible is almost as interesting because of the silence as it is in the conversations. All we are told is that "news spread through the whole town, and many believed in the Lord." This is what I want us to see. One man, fulfilling a simple ministry by reaching out to a lame man, is used by God to impact every resident in at least three communities. These people not only saw something in Peter that was appealing, but they came to the point of realizing they needed what he had to offer.

It's time to begin asking ourselves some questions. In what ways do we minister to others in an appealing way? In other words, what things do we do that will cause others to notice, but beyond simply noticing, they will actually desire what we have?

I'm not suggesting you need to be able to walk up to a lame man, touch him, and cause him to be able to walk. But, what if you are able to reach out to a person with needs and touch them in such a way that makes a difference in their life. Suppose it's a homeless person, or a lonely individual, or a hungry child. In the day-to-day activities of your life, what are the appealing ministries others see?

What I am suggesting is that if this kind of ministry is a part of your life in such a way that others notice, God would put you in places where people will soon find themselves needing what you have. They will move beyond noticing there is something different about you to the point of wanting what it is you have.

Born as the son of a French harness maker, Louis was an unlikely candidate for the notoriety that awaited him. His hometown was the village of Coupvray, not far from the outskirts of Paris. In 1812, at the age of three, Louis was playing in his father's leather shop. As often happens with any three-year-old, Louis disappeared from his father's attention for a few moments. The curious child picked up a sharp knife.

Grasping the shiny blade in his clumsy little hands, the young Louis accidentally slit one of his eyes. It was immediately apparent the eye would never see again. In a time before modern antibiotics, the resulting infection took the vision from Louis' other eye.

For several years, Louis attended the village school with his brothers and sisters. By the time he reached his tenth birthday, his father realized that Louis needed a special education. He was taken to the nearby city of Paris and enrolled in the National Institution for the Blind. Louis excelled as a student, and upon graduation he was asked to remain on campus as an instructor.

Louis always struggled with frail health. A bout with tuberculosis caused him to develop an incessant cough that made it virtually impossible to lecture in a classroom. Finally, he had to give up his position and return home where he died at the relatively young age of forty-two.

Although he lived with blindness for all but the first three years of his life, Louis is best remembered for his vision. As an

11 year-old student at the Institution for the Blind, Louis was introduced to an invention of an officer in Napoleon's army. It was a system of raised dots called "night writing" that was used to send coded messages.

Louis Braille took that military writing system and turned it into a reading method used by the blind. He took something that was quite ordinary and turned it into something that was quite necessary for many people.

When we live as *Unapologetic Ambassadors for Christ* that is exactly what will happen with our faith. What many will think is quite ordinary, even appealing perhaps, will soon become something that is seen as necessary by many people. At that point we have the opportunity to make an amazing impact for Christ in our community.

Reflections:

List an area or a place where you see God working. As you think of that place, reflect on your involvement. Are you in a ministry where it is obvious God is working?

When other people have a need, do they feel comfortable coming to you for help? If not, why?

What are the areas of your spiritual life that are attractive to others?

Respect

One of the great ambassadors for Christ from years past was William Tyndale (c. 1494–1536). He was an English scholar who became a leading figure in the Protestant Reformation. He is best known for his translation of the Bible in English, something which was very rare at the time. Tyndale's translation was the first English Bible to draw directly from Hebrew and Greek texts, the first English one to take advantage of the printing press, and first of the new English Bibles of the Reformation. The reason for the controversy was because it was seen as a direct assault on the Church of England. This new Bible made it difficult for the church to control people.

In 1535, Tyndale was arrested and jailed in a castle outside Brussels for over a year. In 1536 he was convicted of heresy and executed by strangulation, after which his body was burned at the stake, just to add insult.

History records the final words spoken by Tyndale as he was dying. Apparently he spoke with an enthusiastic zeal and a loud voice. He prayed, "Lord! Open the King of England's eyes."

His prayer gives new meaning to the notion that we should love our enemies, since it was the King of England who had Tyndale put to death. However, this death bed prayer seems to have been answered, at least partially, when King Henry authorized a new Bible, known as the Great Bible, for use by the Church of England. This Bible was primarily the work of William Tyndale. The Tyndale Bible, as it was known, played a crucial role in spreading the Reformation across the entire British Empire.

King Henry did not come around to agreeing with William Tyndale's theology. However, he was still motivated to change his thinking about the important issue of biblical translation. Consequently, many good things have come as a result.

There is a captivating story recorded in the book of Daniel about a similar situation.

Then Nebuchadnezzar came as close as he could to the door of the flaming furnace and shouted: "Shadrach, Meshach, and Abednego, servants of the Most High God, come out! Come here!" So Shadrach, Meshach, and Abednego stepped out of the fire.

Then the high officers, officials, governors, and advisers crowded around them and saw that the fire had not touched them. Not a hair on their heads was singed, and their clothing was not scorched. They didn't even smell of smoke!

Then Nebuchadnezzar said, "Praise to the God of Shadrach, Meshach, and Abednego! He sent his angel to rescue his servants who trusted in him. They defied the king's command and were willing to die rather than serve or worship any god except their own God.

Therefore, I make this decree: If any people, whatever their race or nation or language, speak a word against the God of Shadrach, Meshach, and Abednego, they will be torn limb from limb, and their houses will be turned into heaps of rubble. There is no other god who can rescue like this!" (Daniel 3:26-29)

The event described in these verses occurred while God's people were living in a faraway place known as Babylon, separated from their homeland. The king, Nebuchadnezzar, constructed a gold statue that was 90 feet high; that's approximately an eight-story building. He then sent word through all his officials that when a musical note was sounded, everyone was to bow down and worship the statue.

In order to understand and fully appreciate what happened next, we need to understand some background to this event. King Nebuchadnezzar of Babylon led his troops to invade and capture Israel. He then ordered that the finest young men be taken to Babylon to be his servants. Among those men were Daniel (we will learn more about him later), and three others named Hananiah, Mishael, and Azariah. Daniel's three friends were later renamed to Shadrach, Meshach, and Abednego.

These men chose not to eat the food provided by the Babylonians, but to remain faithful and eat according to their religion. They received permission for a short test to prove their food choice was best, and after ten days they were stronger and healthier than the others. God honored their commitment to obedience. Even the King was impressed, and he gave them a special place of respect in his administration.

After a period of time, "the king appointed Shadrach, Meshach, and Abednego to be in charge of all the affairs of the province of Babylon, while Daniel remained in the king's court" (Daniel 2:43). These men were faithful to God, and God responded by placing them in high positions of authority and respect. They were well-liked by Nebuchadnezzar himself.

As was common practice for ancient kings, Nebuchadnezzar constructed the huge statue as incentive for his subjects to worship him. From our perspective it seems quite arrogant, but given the time it was not an uncommon event.

When the time came to sound the instruments and call everyone to worship, God's three servants chose to remain faithful to God's commandment and refused to bow down before the "graven image." As you might expect, not everyone in the King's court was a fan of the three young men. After all, they were probably seen as the teacher's pets, which always elicits jealousy. They quickly went and reported to the King: "They refuse to serve your gods and do not worship the gold statue you have set up" (Daniel 3:12).

You've been there probably. You try to do the right thing, and others come along and jealously undermine your best efforts. Since it has happened to us, we are tempted to keep our mouths shut the next time. We remember what it is like to speak up for the right thing, or to avoid what we know is the wrong thing. If Shadrach, Meshach, and Abednego worked in your office, or tried to get along with the others in your shop, or had to live with your family members they would know how hard it is to remain faithful.

But, you see. They did understand. They knew the King would be true to his word and destroy any who disobeyed his edict. They knew they would not survive if they refused to bow to the idol. Sure enough, we are told that Nebuchadnezzar flew into a rage when he heard what the young men had done, or rather, what they refused to do.

However, the king was willing to give them one more chance. He didn't want to destroy these young men who were so valuable to him, so he said, "Let's try this again."

But the young men told him that it wouldn't matter; they were not going to change their mind. This is what they said, "... we do not need to defend ourselves before you. If we are thrown into the blazing furnace, the God whom we serve is able to save us. He will rescue us from your power, Your Majesty. But even if he doesn't, we want to make it clear to you, Your Majesty, that we will never serve your gods or worship the gold statue you have set up" (Daniel 3:16-18).

You will not be surprised to learn that the King was so angry now that his "face was distorted with rage." I'm not sure I've ever seen anyone that mad. There was no stopping him at this point. These three young men were goners. The furnace used for capital punishment was heated to seven times its normal roasting temperature. In fact, it was so hot that several of the executioners assigned to throw people into the fire were consumed by the heat. There would be no surviving this execution.

Nebuchadnezzar was eager to see this execution first-hand so he watched the fire from a distance. What he saw was stunning and confusing. He would have expected the three to be instantly consumed by the flames, but instead he saw four men walking around inside the furnace, unbound, and unharmed. The unnamed fourth man appeared to be a god according to the King himself.

Now, this man who had gone from having a distorted face because of his anger to having a perplexed expression on his face, called out the three young men by name. He instructed them to come out of the furnace. As they stepped out of the fire, everyone crowded around them and noticed that neither their hair nor clothing was singed by the enormous heat. In fact, we are given the added detail that there was not even the smell of smoke on them.

Then Nebuchadnezzar said,

"Praise to the God of Shadrach, Meshach, and Abednego! He sent his angel to rescue his servants who trusted in him. They defied the king's command and were willing to die rather than serve or worship any god except their own God. Therefore, I make this decree: If any people, whatever their race or nation or language, speak a word against the God of Shadrach, Meshach, and Abednego, they will be torn limb from limb, and their houses will be turned into heaps of rubble. There is no other god who can rescue like this!" Then the king promoted Shadrach, Meshach, and Abednego to even higher positions in the province of Babylon. (Daniel 3:28-30)

I want to point out a few things that we learn from this experience that relate to our lives in the modern world.

The Witness

The three Hebrew young men provided a powerful witness with their faithfulness to God. They knew what God wanted from them, and they were willing to live according to His call. By the way, this was even in the midst of a very hostile environment. It was not a matter of attending Sunday morning service without telling your friends and co-workers. They actually refused to bow down before another god when everyone else in the nation was doing it.

This is the kind of witness provided by an *Unapologetic Ambassador of Christ.* They did not attempt to argue their way out of the situation. I suspect they could have appealed to the King based on the success of their previous work, or just because he liked them for some reason. They did not go to the courts and seek some kind of exemption, or appeal to the Human Resources Department that they should be excused.

All they did was publicly live out their faith, even though it put them at odds with everyone else in their world.

What I think is the most striking element of their statement of faith needs to be mentioned. Notice what they said as they were confronted to renounce their faith: "If we are thrown into the blazing furnace, the God whom we serve is able to save us. He will rescue us from your power, Your Majesty. But even if he doesn't, we want to make it clear to you, Your Majesty, that we will never serve your gods or worship the gold statue you have set up" (Daniel 3:17-18).

Did you catch that? They declared the belief that God would rescue them, and then added, even if He does not, we will still serve Him. Amazing words. Their belief in God was so sure that even if they were wrong about their hopes, they would continue to be true to Him. This is perhaps the strongest statement of faith recorded in scripture. We praise the father who prayed, "I do believe, but help me overcome my unbelief!" (Mark 9:24), but it was pretty weak compared to these young men.

The Effect

I'm sure these words echoed through King Nebuchadnezzar's head as he saw the men walking around inside the furnace, and as he called them out, and as he touched their unharmed clothing and shook their barely warm hands. It was a witness he would never forget. Then he issued another edict. This time it was not about his statue or his idol. It was about the God of Shadrach, Meshach, and Abednego. He declared that if anyone in the kingdom should utter a disparaging word about this God that they would be torn limb from limb.

How things changed! All of a sudden it went from living in fear of death for worshipping God to living in fear of death for speaking ill of God. This is the power of giving a witness on behalf of God. Not only was Nebuchadnezzar's mind changed, but also his actions. We have no indication that his heart was actually changed. He did not suddenly become a believer and follower of Israel's God, but he did become a respecter of God.

The Response

King Nebuchadnezzar declared that there is no god who can rescue like this god. He then elevated the three young men to even higher positions in his administration. It's interesting to note that Nebuchadnezzar did not personally put his trust in God; neither did he become an obedient servant. There is no indication that he constructed a temple where he could worship the God of the Israelites.

However, he did recognize the reality and power of God. Even if he was not a servant of God, he was a respecter of God.

This was an amazing transformation for a man who had recently constructed a ninety-foot tall idol and commanded the worship of the people.

This is a crucial concept in today's world. There is something about the way modern-day Christians are living that often causes the exact opposite to occur. What I mean is that many have lost all respect for God, ignoring His commands, using His name as a swear word, making fun of His followers. It indicates to me that we, as His ambassadors, are doing something wrong. Unlike the three young men in Babylon, others are not looking at our life and coming to a place of respect for God.

Numerous changes in the past few generations demonstrate the loss of respect for God. It was not that long ago that...

- stores and restaurants were closed on Sunday
- school programs and activities were comfortable with prayer and religious symbols
- holidays maintained their specifically religious purpose (i.e. Christmas and Easter)
- youth and children's activities were not scheduled on Sunday (or often, not even on Wednesday evening)
- pastors were viewed with respect

This list could certainly be lengthened, but the point I want to make is that as ambassadors for Christ, we have done something wrong to cause people to lose respect for God.

There is a great need for more people like Shadrach, Meshach, and Abednego who will live out their faith, even in the face of death. We need more people like William Tyndale who are not ashamed to pray for those who are opposed to the faith.

We need many more *Unapologetic Ambassadors for Christ*—men and women who will live their lives in such a manner that even if others chose not to follow Jesus, they will still have great respect for God.

Reflections:

What spiritual disciplines do you practice that are noticed by others? Are you committed to them even if there is opposition or ridicule?

Describe a time in your life when you had to trust God even though you were unsure of the outcome.

Admiration and Awe

As a pastor, it is not unusual for someone to come up to me and ask for prayer. It might be someone I encounter at church, or perhaps a phone call, text, or email. Most of the time these prayer requests come from folks I know and who are also followers of Jesus and believers in prayer.

However, on occasion, I will get a request to pray from someone who is not a believer in Christ. It is most likely because they are facing a difficult time such as sickness or death, or perhaps a loved one is in trouble and needs immediate help. I love to pray for people, especially those who specifically ask, but it might seem odd for a non-believer to ask for prayer.

I realize many of these requests come to me because they know I'm a preacher, but I suspect you also get similar requests. It should not surprise us to hear that non-believers turn to our God when they are in trouble.

This truth is revealed in the story of Daniel in the lion's den. This is much more than a children's story. This is a great story of living as an *Unapologetic Ambassador for Christ* (read Daniel 6).

Daniel was an Israelite living in captivity in Babylon. He had been specifically chosen, along with others like the three young men we discussed in the previous chapter, to serve in the court of the king. Daniel had distinguished himself to the extent that Darius, the king, named him an administrator to supervise other designated leaders over the entire kingdom. Daniel excelled even more, and Darius made plans to name him ruler over the entire kingdom.

This is where the political intrigue began. As you would expect, there were others who coveted this position especially not wanting it to be given to an Israelite, an outsider, or as we might say today, an immigrant. They hired private detectives, and followed Daniel's every move in order to catch him doing something that would disqualify him from the position, "but they couldn't find anything to criticize or condemn. He was faithful, always responsible, and completely trustworthy" (Daniel 6:4).

What do you do when your enemy has no faults? Imagine trying to win an election when there is no way to criticize your opponent. These men didn't give up. They devised a plan that was sure to work. They came up with a plan to use Daniel's faithfulness to God against him.

They went to the king with an idea they knew would appeal to his ego. They recommended that he enact a law forbidding anyone from praying to anyone other than the king for thirty days. They even went a step further, and specified that the punishment for breaking the law would require being thrown into a den of lions—in other words, capital punishment. They even suggested the king take some kind of oath, making it an official law of the "Medes and Persians" (see Daniel 6:8).

With his ego appropriately stroked, King Darius followed their advice and decreed that it was now illegal to pray to anyone other than him. I'm curious as to how he expected to be able to answer the prayers of others, but that is not really a part of the story.

Daniel's enemies were confident enough to know that an edict from the king would not be sufficient to keep him from praying. In fact, they were counting on his faithfulness to God in order for their plan to work. And they were correct.

Obedient

There are three qualities of Daniel's faith that made it possible for him to be unapologetic before others. First, he was obedient. Daniel's pattern was to pray three times each day facing the city of Jerusalem. There is not anything in scripture to indicate God prescribed three prayers per day, or the necessity to pray toward Jerusalem, so let's not make too much of it. Perhaps he was like the Psalmist who prayed "morning, noon, and night" when he was in distress (see Psalm 55:17). Also, it might be that his heart longed for Jerusalem, the home of his people, and the location of God's temple.

The point is that Daniel prayed like this as a means of obedience and faithfulness to God. In fact, it is what got him in trouble in the first place. Others noticed the strength of his obedience, and that is how they attacked him. They knew, in spite of a new law, Daniel would remain obedient.

We noted earlier in this book that one of the problems that keep us from being *Unapologetic Ambassadors for God* is our lack of obedience. We must learn the truth and then obey the truth.

Consistent

But when Daniel learned that the law had been signed, he went home and knelt down as usual in his upstairs room, with its windows open toward Jerusalem. He prayed three times a day, just as he had always done, giving thanks to his God. (Daniel 6:10)

I want you to notice two phrases in this verse that describe the consistency of Daniel's faith and actions. We are told that he knelt down to pray as "usual." The next sentence says that he prayed "just as he had always done..."

Nothing changed for Daniel, in spite of the new law. In spite of enemies who were out to destroy him. In spite of the possibility of being hurled into a den of hungry lions, he continued doing what he had always done.

You know how some days you feel on top of the world spiritually, and other days you feel like the Holy Spirit has left without a forwarding address. All of us ride the roller coaster of faith, some have more peaks and valleys than others, but we all experience the ups and downs. Such was not the case with Daniel.

It would be easy for Daniel to ask to be excused from his normal spiritual exercises, at least for a few weeks, just until this whole thing blew over, but he didn't ask. He continued with his obedience just like he had always done. The outer circumstances may change, but the inner consistency kept him on target.

Transparent

OK, Daniel, if you are going to break the law, at least pull down the shades, and do it behind closed doors. There's no need to break the law out in the open where everyone can see you. But, he did. The text very clearly says that he prayed to God with the windows open. He allowed the world to see that he remained faithful to God, even under threat of arrest and death.

This is consistent with the way Daniel had always lived. Apparently he always prayed in such a manner that the world could see. That is why his opponents knew where he was vulnerable.

In order to be an *Unapologetic Ambassador for Christ*, our faith and obedience must be visible. God is not honored by closet Christians. The cause of Christ is not advanced by followers who hide their faith. People are not drawn to faith when our faith is only practiced behind darkened windows. We need to allow people to see the hope that is within us.

Daniel's detractors wasted no time. The first time they observed him praying we are told that they went "straight to the king" in order to turn him in. Now they had him just where they wanted him. The king had been talked into establishing a law, and now he would be forced to uphold his own law. Daniel would be thrown into a den of hungry lions for lunch.

Once the king confirmed that he would enforce his new law, he was informed that his friend Daniel was guilty. Now listen to what it says:

Hearing this, the king was deeply troubled, and he tried to think of a way to save Daniel. He spent the rest of the day looking for a way to get Daniel out of this predicament. (Daniel 6:14)

The king spent the entire day trying to come up with a solution to the problem he had created. He didn't want to kill Daniel. He had great respect for the man. In fact, this enormous respect led to the jealousy that eventually precipitated this whole situation.

However, he was unsuccessful in coming up with a solution. Daniel's enemies returned that evening to press the matter. They knew the king was in an impossible situation, or as they say, between a rock and a hard place. He would have to follow through and have Daniel executed by the lions.

We have now come to the verse that serves as the basis for this entire chapter. It describes the action of king Darius as he realized there was no way to spare Daniel.

So at last the king gave orders for Daniel to be arrested and thrown into the den of lions. The king said to him, "May your God, whom you serve so faithfully, rescue you." (Daniel 6:16)

He did what he had to do and had Daniel arrested and thrown to the lions. But, note carefully what he said to Daniel. He encouraged him with the words of hope that perhaps Daniel's God would save him.

Remember, this is a man who had just issued an edict requiring everyone in the nation pray to him. This is not some kind of personal statement of faith. He was not accepting for himself the reality and power of God. Instead, he was simply hoping that his good friend Daniel would be spared by his God. Daniel had lived his life so that others, whether they believed in his God or not, would be confident that his God would get him out of whatever he was going through.

Here is an amazing fact to help us appreciate the power of Daniel's faith. Ancient history records that king Darius was a strong believer in the religion of Zoroastrianism, and he felt that the god Ahura Mazda had appointed him king. In other words, he did not believe in the true God himself, but he knew that Daniel's God would take care of Daniel.

That is exactly the type of admiration that comes to an *Unapologetic Ambassador for Christ*. We are to live in such a way that even if people don't fall on their knees and proclaim Jesus as their savior, they are at least confident He is capable of saving us. Do people believe this about your God? Do they see His power in your life? Are you living in such a way that others recognize the power of God even if they do not accept Him for themselves?

However, the story of Daniel and king Darius doesn't end yet.

A stone was brought and placed over the mouth of the den. The king sealed the stone with his own royal seal and the seals of his nobles, so that no one could rescue Daniel. Then the king returned to his palace and spent the night fasting. He refused his usual entertainment and couldn't sleep at all that night. (Daniel 6:17-18)

Daniel was tossed into the cave with the hungry lions, a massive stone was placed over the opening, and the seal of the king of other leaders was affixed to insure that it would not be opened. Yet, the king did not walk away in despair because he had just killed his friend Daniel. Instead, he spent the night fasting, hoping, and praying for Daniel's survival. He had already expressed the hope that Daniel's God would rescue him, now he waited for it to happen.

Remember, this is a man who was not a believer and follower of Daniel's God. In fact, secular history records that Darius credited his success to one of the pagan gods worshiped at the time. He was not a closet believer in the God of the Jews, yet he still hoped that something good would happen.

Early the next morning, Darius rushed out to the lions' den, and called upon his guard to roll away the stone that sealed the entrance. You could probably hear the desperation in his voice as he called out, "Daniel, servant of the living God! Was your God, whom you serve so faithfully, able to rescue you from the lions?" (Daniel 6:20).

I love the way the story teller describes Daniel's response.

Daniel answered, "Long live the king! My God sent his angel to shut the lions' mouths so that they would not hurt me, for I have been found innocent in his sight. And I have not wronged you, Your Majesty." (Daniel 6:21)

You can almost hear the cockiness in Daniel's words as he described what God had done for him. There was no need to worry or fear, he was innocent of any wrong doing so he knew God would protect him. He was certainly unapologetic in his witness to Darius and the entire kingdom about the strength and goodness of God.

We have already seen how Darius, who did not believe in Daniel's God, respected Daniel enough to recognize God's potential. However, now he goes one step further. Daniel's walk looked so good that other people who don't even believe in God encouraged others to tremble, worship, and fear your God. Listen to the king's proclamation:

> *Then King Darius sent this message to the people of every*
> *race and nation and language throughout the world: "Peace*
> *and prosperity to you! "I decree that everyone throughout my*
> *kingdom should tremble with fear before the God of Daniel.*
> *For he is the living God,*
> *and he will endure forever.*
> *His kingdom will never be destroyed,*
> *and his rule will never end.*
> *He rescues and saves his people;*
> *he performs miraculous signs and wonders*
> *in the heavens and on earth.*
> *He has rescued Daniel*
> *from the power of the lions."* (Daniel 6:25-27)

There are several basic things we learn from Daniel. How you live your life should be so good people will say I want what you have. This thing called Christianity I want some of that. They might not understand much about the Christian faith, but when they look at our life they should be drawn to something about us, something we possess that they want for themselves.

Jesus identified us as the "salt" and "light" of the world. Daniel was salt and light, out-classing others. He was out-shining everyone else. He was the number one person. It was so obvious that the king put him in charge of the whole kingdom.

He did not let an action or attitude mess up his strength and disqualify him for what God had in store for him. They could not find anything on Daniel. We want people to stay out of our closet because they will find something. Not so with Daniel. When we are elevated because of living God's way, there will be those who hate us, even hating our relationship with Christ.

Even though the king threw Daniel in the lions' den, he hoped God would save him. It teaches us that people should have confidence in our relationship with God in spite of their lack of a relationship with God themselves—a sinner reminding others of the power of our God.

Your relationship can cause someone else to make an accurate statement about God (v.25). Your lions' den is not for you; it is an opportunity to proclaim a great truth about God. Where you are in your trials and tribulations is a testimony that God will change a person's life. The salt will not change a culture, but your lifestyle will cause others to understand God.

Your lifestyle is the loudest testimony you will ever live. Daniel's consistent walk with God is what spoke. How many people can say you are loyal to God? How many people can look at your Facebook profile and say this person is loyal to God.

You cannot separate your Christian walk from who you are. Daniel's environment was very much anti-God, but it did not have an effect on his prayer life. His lifestyle was strong, an accurate reflection of his faith. The weaker the lifestyle the less threat we are. Your lifestyle comes out of your obedience to God, and the depth of obedience is based on the depth of your love for God. The more you love him the more you look to obey Him.

Just as light travels faster than sound, so to does what people see in you affect them quicker than what they hear come out of your mouth. Therefore, our message as the church has to change from concentrating on preaching to concentrating on living. The world doesn't want to hear us, but they will have no choice other than to watch our lifestyle.

The dictionary defines lifestyle as being made up of your habits, your attitudes, your taste, your moral standards, and your economic level, that together, constitute the mode of living of an individual or group.

So let's break down lifestyle. Your lifestyle is reflected in your habits. Habits are something a person does often in a regular repeated way. This tends to happen unconsciously because you have done it for so long. Because it happens regularly and for so long it is usually done easily. Habits are acquired and learned. The habits of a Christian have to be acquired in such a way that speaks of a lifestyle that studies the Word of God. To do certain things like pray, give thanks, be gracious, or willing to respond to injustice should come easily for us.

Daniel habitually did the things God led him to do. Consequently others noticed and lives were impacted. The same will be true for you and me when we come to the point of doing the things of God habitually, and they come to define our lifestyle. It is at that point we become *Unapologetic Ambassadors for Christ*.

Another factor is attitude. My father taught me that "attitude determines approach and approach determines success or failure." Your attitude is a settled way of thinking about someone or something. A person's attitude tends to tell what's going on in a persons heart. It reflects a persons behavior. Zig Ziglar said "Your attitude not your aptitude, will determine your altitude." It is your attitude that will determine where you go in life.

People ask me if I ever imagined doing what I am doing. I tell them we all imagine our futures. The difference for some is this imagination that ignites a belief in us. This causes them to believe in such a way that puts them on a path subconsciously towards achieving what they imagined.

To imagine as Christians means to allow your relationship with Christ to govern the way you imagine. This will cause a person to first seek the will of God for their future. This will allow for their plans to always include glorifying God. This concept is important to the life of a Christian. Too often, people put the ownership of ministry on the pastor because they don't believe that their vocation is a ministry.

And now, dear brothers and sisters, one final thing. Fix your thoughts on what is true, and honorable, and right, and pure, and lovely, and admirable. Think about things that are excellent and worthy of praise. (Philippians 4:8)

This Scripture is the blueprint for "thinking in Christian," so let's break it down. This blueprint is based on the premise of filling your mind with things that would give you the desire to worship God. It also pushes one to commit to service to people; thinking leads to actions. Every action is tied to a thought. Christ said that a sinful thought (i.e. lust in your heart) is the equivalent of committing the sin. Thought is where it starts and when the thought is not dealt with it goes to the heart.

What is *true*, talks about Christ. He said in scriptures that He is the truth. The fact that if we are searching for truth we would understand that real truth is found in Christ.

What is *honorable*, deals with the whole notion of honesty. To think honestly allows you to focus on truths about you and who you really are. This will keep you in a healthy balance of humility. This is the part that will help you in good tasteful behavior.

What is *right* (just), talks more about righteousness. I have been taught that righteousness means, being in right standing with God. So to think in Christian is a thought pattern and process that allows you to be in right standing with God.

What is *pure*, deals with the cleanliness of the thought. What are the motives behind what you are thinking? Why are you thinking what you are thinking? Is what you are thinking going to glorify God or serve the people? This process is to help people from getting caught in selfishness and lean towards selflessness. All sin has its origin in selfishness.

What is *lovely*, and what is *admirable* is making sure the time you use to think adds value to your life and is worth admiring. When you think this way, stir up a wonder in your mind that you would want God to approve. To have admirable thinking, is to go through a process of esteeming oneself. It is also to have thinking that will reverence God.

Reflections:

Under the following terms, describe how your life is...

Obedient

Consistent

Transparent

Conclusion

A sizable number of young women in our society are suffering from conditions labeled anorexia and bulimia. An anorexic person thinks she is fat, even though it might not be a reality, and becomes obsessed with losing weight. Because of this obsession, she will go on diets and fasts, literally starving herself to the point of death. The bulimic person gorges herself, feels guilty, and then forces herself to regurgitate to keep from gaining weight. It does not matter how thin a person is in reality, they perceive themselves as being overweight.

Christian counselor Bob George tells the story of Janet. She had been under treatment for six weeks in a leading hospital in Dallas. Their approach was to help her improve her self-image. They taught her to practice Hindu meditation techniques in order to improve her self-esteem. After six weeks of this approach, her parents removed her from the hospital and brought her to George for help. In one week she went home completely cured.

The key was not George's tremendous counseling techniques, but his directing her to the truth of her condition. He first determined that she was in fact a Christian. However, she had accepted the lie promoted by the world that to be accepted and worthwhile you must fit a certain physical mold. (i.e. look at what we are constantly told on television and in advertisements.) Using God's Word, George showed Janet how she was loved and accepted by God, and that in Christ she was righteous and capable. Once she began living by the truth, rather than the lies of society, she was free from her terrible bondage.

This example of Janet and her terrible condition illustrates what I think is probably the greatest threat to Christian living—the failure to know and live according to the truth. Many Christians are in bondage to falsehoods. You know many of these folks, those who are...

- unable to effectively serve Christ because of the lie that they are not worthy or capable,
- judgmental of other Christians because of the lie that their own lifestyle is the only one acceptable to God,
- constantly frustrated because of the lie that certain habits and destructive behaviors cannot be overcome,
- tired and worn out by an exhaustive schedule because of the lie that successful people must accomplish many things,
- discouraged and depressed because of the lie that something bad is destined to happen.

We easily recognize the lie that had enslaved Janet and her eating patterns. However, it is not so easy to identify the lie that enslaves us.

An *Unapologetic Ambassador for Christ* is one who has arranged life according to the truth. Living according to the truth sets us free. If we want to enjoy all of the blessings of the Christian life then we must learn to orchestrate our life around the truth found in God's Word. Overcoming the power of deceit in our lives is possible through Jesus. The truth has the power to set us free if we learn to live according to its precepts.

In order to successfully live according to the truth then we must first understand the process of arriving at this position. The first step is to the know the truth. Obviously it is impossible to live according to truth when the truth is unknown. Jesus tells us how to know the truth—by "abiding in My word" (John 8:31-32).

The truth about life is found in God's Word. Unless you know the Bible then you do not know the truth. In John 17:17, speaking to His father, Jesus said, "Thy word is truth." Therefore, whatever God's Word says about life is the truth that will lead us to freedom.

However, it is not enough to know the truth. This passage does not say, "You shall know the truth and knowledge shall make you free." Knowledge does not lead to freedom, truth makes us free. We are set free by the truth when we "abide." To abide in Jesus means to adhere to His teachings. It is to direct our lives on the basis of the truth. In other words, it is to live according to the truth.

The process is very simple. Learn the truth and then live according to the truth. The predominant belief in our world today is that truth is relevant. Have you ever heard anyone declare, "That may be true for you but it is not true for me!" What they are saying is that there really is no objective truth, it all depends upon the individual and the situation. The world today denies the existence of objective standards.

It is not surprising that Christians have failed to order their lives around the truth coming out of this society and this kind of teaching. We hesitate claiming to have found the truth when everyone else says it cannot be found, there is no such thing.

There was a recent article that details some of the problems with the American educational system. The author gave shocking statistics about illiteracy among High School, and even college graduates. It should concern us that our children are growing up without learning to read and write. However, it should be of even greater concern that Christians are living a lifetime without ever learning the truth about life.

Let me give you something we could call a Spiritual Aptitude Test. The first question: What is God's opinion of me? The objective truth is that if you are not a Christian then He loves you and gave His Son for you. If you are a Christian then He sees you as totally righteous and holy in Christ. If you have the opinion that God sees you as a worthless sinner or even a sinner saved by grace then you have believed a lie.

The second question: Are those who are active in church more acceptable to God? The answer is no because we can only be acceptable to God by being in Christ.

The third question: Can a Christian expect to have joy every day? The answer is yes because joy is not dependent upon circumstances but our relationship with Christ.

We need to immerse ourselves in the Word of God, learn the truth, and then live according to that truth rather than falsehoods. Truth has tremendous power in our lives. It has the potency to defeat the three greatest enemies that we face. Truth will enable us to be set free from death. In John 14, Jesus spoke of going on to heaven to prepare the way for his followers. Then he declares, I am the way, and the truth, and the life; no one comes to the father, but through me (John. 14:6). To live according to the truth gives us entrance into heaven, and defeat of the ultimate enemy of death. The truth sets us free from eternal damnation and the punishment of God's wrath.

Truth also sets us free from Satan. The source of all lies is Satan.

> *"You are of your father the devil, and you want to do the desires of your father. He was a murderer from the beginning, and does not stand in the truth, because there is no truth in him. Whenever he speaks a lie, he speaks from his own nature; for he is a liar, and the father of lies." (John. 8:44)*

Satan strives to enslave us by filling our minds with lies. The very first sin was committed because Eve believed Satan's lie, "You surely shall not die" (Genesis 3:4). Every lie has its source in Satan. He is the "Father of (all) lies." When we choose to live according to truth then we are set free from Satan's lies. He loses his ability to manipulate and control us. He loses his power to destroy our lives. One of our greatest resources in spiritual warfare is truth. Our spiritual armor consists of the belt of truth (see Ephesians 6:14).

Finally, truth sets us free from sin. When Jesus prayed for His disciples he prayed, sanctify them in the truth (John. 17:17). To be sanctified means to be set apart, to be separated from sin. Sanctification is accomplished by the truth. "You were running well; who hindered you from obeying the truth?" (Galatians 5:7)

Sanctification, righteousness, purity; all of these are the result of living according to the truth. The vast majority of problems we experience in our lives are the result of either not knowing or not living according to the truth. People have had fun with the little saying, "God says it, I believe it, and that settles it" for years. However, it would be more effective to say, "God says it, I believe it, I live by it, and that settles it." The truth has the power to set you free from all of those problems and continuing sins that bring you frequent defeat. The truth has the power to set you apart from the staining influences of the world. The truth has the power to enable you to live out the righteousness that you already possess in Christ.

It is imperative that we understand the practical implications of living according to the truth. The truth can have a profound effect upon every aspect of our lives. There are two lies which dominate Christian efforts and activities. The first is the lie that "I can't do anything." Many Christians are characterized by complete inactivity in their Christian lives because they have believed the lie that they are incapable of any good thing. The old hymn, "At the Cross" contained the phrase "Would he devote that sacred head for such a worm as I?" There are a lot of "worm Christians" who have accepted the lie that they are worthless.

The second lie, and the exact opposite is that "I am capable." On the other end of the spectrum are those Christians who believe they can do anything they put their mind to. They are very self-confident, and usually very active.

Both of these concepts are false. The truth is found in Philippians 4:13 that says, "I can do all things through Christ who strengthens me." Our own efforts are futile but if we make ourselves available to Christ then we can do anything. This truth motivates the "worm Christian" and it redirects the active Christian.

The truth gives us victory over having to live the Christian life according to our own strength and ability.

Another very practical struggle for Christians is in the area of negative emotions. When it comes to fear, the lie is that we should be afraid of faltering finances, or deteriorating health. Life is full of so many uncertainties that our only recourse is to fear the possibilities. When we believe that lie then we will be spiritually impotent.

> *"That is why I tell you not to worry about everyday life— whether you have enough food and drink, or enough clothes to wear. Isn't life more than food, and your body more than clothing? Look at the birds. They don't plant or harvest or store food in barns, for your heavenly Father feeds them. And aren't you far more valuable to him than they are? Can all your worries add a single moment to your life? (Matthew 6:25-27)*

Another emotion that can cause us to struggle is anger. The lie is that we have been unjustly wronged, and our anger toward others is righteous. The lie is that in this instance it is right to harbor anger toward our terrible enemies.

> *And don't sin by letting anger control you. Don't let the sun go down while you are still angry, for anger gives a foothold to the devil. (Ephesians 4:26-27)*

The truth sets us free from these destructive feelings and fears.

A third very practical struggle experienced by most Christians is in the area of personal encounters and relationships. It is amazing how many lies we believe about other people. It often appears that we would rather believe a lie than make the effort to discover the truth. It always astounds me to hear two different people tell their version of the same incident. It is almost as if they witnessed two different incidents. We must not allow our opinions of others to be clouded by lies and misunderstandings.

Another area of difficulty is that we are so quick to judge motives. For example, If someone does not speak to us at church we might think it is because they do not like us, or if someone does not help us with an activity it is because they think we are wrong, or if someone disagrees with us it is because they are narrow-minded and judgmental, or if someone does not participate in a project it is because they are uncaring and indifferent.

Scripture has so much to say concerning the truth of relationships. If we would relate to one another according to God's Word then our relationships would be a source of joy rather than sorrow.

> *Get rid of all bitterness, rage, anger, harsh words, and slander, as well as all types of evil behavior. Instead, be kind to each other, tenderhearted, forgiving one another, just as God through Christ has forgiven you. (Ephesians 4:31-32)*

The truth has many possibilities which are available to anyone who will live according to its precepts. We need the attitude of the Psalmist in our desire for the truth:

> *Lead me in thy truth and teach me. (Psalm 25:5)*

> *For thy lovingkindness is before my eyes, and I have walked in thy truth. (Psalm 26:3)*

Thy lovingkindness and thy truth will continually preserve me. (Psalm 40:11)

Teach me thy way, O Lord; I will walk in thy truth. (Psalm 86:11)

Remove the false way from me and graciously grant me thy law. (Psalm 119:29)

Just as you could not become a Christian on your own, neither can you be a Christian on your own. The truth is that Jesus living in you can make all things possible. If you struggle with failure, fear, feelings, financial problems, or faulty relationships then it is evidence that Jesus Christ is not living your life for you; you are doing it yourself.

I have been crucified with Christ; and it is no longer I who live, but Christ lives in me; and the life which I now life in the flesh I live by faith in the son of God, who loved me, and delivered himself up for me. (Galatians 2:20)

When we accept the truth about Jesus, and arrange our lives according to that truth, and live each day according to that truth, we then become *Unapologetic Ambassadors for Christ*. At that point, it is not something we do or accomplish; rather it is simply who we are. Christ living through us will be the everyday experience of our lives.

Christ represented by unapologetic ambassadors becomes a powerful force for changing the world. It is what the first century experienced after the resurrection of Jesus and Pentecost revelation of the Holy Spirit. It is what our world especially needs today. It is certainly needed in your community.

You are now ready to make an impact for Christ in the world. People will know who you represent and who you serve. Your life will be an open book to describe the goodness and mercy of God. People will see and know Jesus because they have known you. They will realize that you are 100 percent Christian, inside and out.

Reflections:

Name three (3) things you discovered about yourself while reading this book.

Would you describe yourself as an *Unapologetic Ambassador for Christ*? If not, what can you do to make that possible?

Share this book with someone you think will benefit.

CPSIA information can be obtained
at www.ICGtesting.com
Printed in the USA
BVOW03s1320131116
467703BV00002B/2/P